THE BENEFITS OF NEUTRAL THINKING

Also by N. Dao

Home Away From Home: a memoir about fleeing Vietnam and growing up in America.

The Flight Attendant: the ghost of a murdered flight attendant gets revenge on the people who killed her onboard an airborne jumbo jet.

Come Back To Me: a story of love, loss, regret – and past life regression.

Contents

The Benefits Of Neutral Thinking ~ page 1
Why Wait? ~ page 3
A Buddhist Thought ~ page 12
On The Job Sight ~ page 13
Fence Sitters Wanted ~ page 17
Gracias, Barcelona *Policia_* ~ page 33
Gracias, Barcelona Bystanders ~ page 44
Captain Cuckoo ~ page 53
"I'm Ready To Go!" ~ page 59
Neutrally Naturally_ ~ page 62
Neutrally, Man-Made ~ page 66
A Few More ~ page 73
Neutral Positioning ~ page 80
Some More Fence Sitting ~ page 87
Neutral and Calm ~ page 91
Onward and Upward to Machu Pichu – part 1 ~ page 92
Onward and Upward to Machu Pichu – part 2 ~ page 103
For The Sake Of Society ~ page 135
Don't Get In The Car With Him ~ page 154
Thanks For Being Late! ~ page 162
Jumping To Conclusions ~ page 164
What Was That? ~ page 166
Amber Alert ~ page 173
My Foibles ~ page 181

The Benefits Of Neutral Thinking

You might have heard of the power of positive thinking.

You might have even heard of the power of negative thinking.

But have you heard of the power of neutral thinking – or to be more accurate – the benefits of neutral thinking?

Probably not. That might be because you're kind of like me. You've witnessed the power of neutral thinking, yet you didn't notice its benefits.

Naturally, you're probably asking right now: *What the heck is neutral thinking?*

Good question.

One good way to define neutral thinking is to differentiate it from its two polar opposite cousins – positive thinking and negative thinking.

Positive thinking is having the perception that the outcome will be in your favor.

Negative thinking is having the perception that the outcome will *not* be in your favor.

As you might have guessed, neutral thinking is the general midpoint in between. It's a state of mind that seeks an equilibrium. It's an objective that tries to be even-handed. It's an outlook that strives for a nuanced balance.

By the way, one facet of neutral thinking is taking the time to gather more information before coming to a definite conclusion, so just by pausing to ask: *What the heck is neutral thinking?* – you've essentially just exercised neutral thinking.

What's more, I'll bet you already apply neutral thinking to your everyday life. When you take a shower, do you turn on only the cold water? I'm guessing you don't unless there's an unusual reason for it. (Libido too lively, is it?) I'll bet you don't use only the hot water either because you know better than to scald yourself. Of course you don't use solely the cold water or the hot water. You're a sensible person who wants a temperature that feels right. You want an intermediate setting between freezing cold and scalding hot. In other words, you want a neutral temperature: *Warm.*

When you think about it, this concept of finding a point of equilibrium is nothing new. As a matter of fact, it's already ingrained in our culture. That's why we have the adage that advises, "All things in moderation." While some of the perks of neutral thinking can be obvious, some can be hidden from the forefront. That's why a bit of scrutiny could be of use. That's why a bit of searching and surveying can help us gain the benefits of neutral thinking.

Why Wait?

Conventional thinking can be convenient, and the ease of convenience can sometimes take us down a road that fails to recognize objective, neutral thinking. A prime example of this is when a gifted, high school athlete is offered two paths. One path takes him from high school straight into professional sports. The other path dictates that he goes to college first and get a degree before he can enter professional sports.

More often than not, conventional thinking dictates that going from high school straight into professional sports is a bad idea. Conventional thinking urges that young athletes go to college first to get an education so they can have something to fall back on in case their sports career takes a downward turn. In other words, conventional thinking counsels high school graduates to wade through four more years of schooling before grabbing that hefty, professional paycheck. Whenever I hear this, I just want to shout out, "Why wait?"

At the time of this writing, there's a basketball player who's in the news. He's poised to go from high school straight into professional sports. I was going to reference him by name, but since I don't know him personally and am not sure how he'd feel about me shining the spotlight on him, I'll hold off on that. I'll just utilize a descriptive method instead. Since he did graduate from high school, I'll refer to him as "Mr. Graduate."

What's special about Mr. Graduate is that he's an immigrant from The Republic Of Congo in Africa. His father died when he was still a toddler, forcing his mother to scrimp together a meager existence for her sons by selling the sparse coffee beans and vegetables that the family was able to grow on their small plot of land – all the while living in fear of the raging war that threatened their safety. Mr. Graduate came to America as a refugee and honed his natural talents to become a top basketball prospect. He was so good that by the time he graduated high school, he was offered $1,200,000 for one year of his time and effort on a professional team.

A practical person would think that everyone would tell him to accept the offer right away. Yet, there were those who adhered to the bondage of conventional thinking and preferred that he cast the big payday aside. Strangely, they advised that he go to college first before accepting a life-altering windfall.

Why?

Let's be objective about this and apply a real-world analysis.

What is the purpose of getting a job? The answers can vary, but one common denominator is undeniable. The purpose of a job is to make money, and all of us must have money in order to live.

Living requires eating – and to eat, we need money to buy food. Sitting down at the dinner table and hardly seeing anything on it is not a welcome sight. I can personally attest to this fact because my family also felt the fallout of war, and there were times when our dinner table was far from picture perfect.

The argument for money to buy food is the same argument for money to acquire many of the other necessities in life, like shelter and clothing. Have you ever been homeless? At one point, our family essentially was, and I can assure you that not having a home can wreak havoc upon the psychological well-being of a family. The result can be stress that creates rancor, and that rancor that can have physical consequences. When the "Great Recession" hit the economy around 2008, I read a news article that said when the economy goes down, the rate of child abuse goes up. I wasn't surprised to hear that. My personal experience has told me that when the hard times hit, the actual physical hits can also be hard.

The naysayers might say I'm being too dire in my depictions. If I am, I'm doing it to make clear how stark the straits can be. Can those same naysayers guarantee that Mr. Graduate won't have to face disastrous hardships if he turns down a sizable payday? Unless they can predict the future with 100% accuracy, they can't justify telling a young man to turn down a gargantuan paycheck that will go a long way in providing for himself and his family.

I think you know by now that when I'm talking about money, I'm talking about it as a tool of necessity – not as a manifestation of greed. I bring this up because some might say that it's greedy for Mr. Graduate to jump at the chance to make $1,200,000. From where I'm standing, I wouldn't say it's a matter of greed. I'd say it's a matter of wise practicality.

As I mentioned, I don't know Mr. Graduate personally. Even so, given the similarities between his background and mine, I would say that, in a way, I definitely know where he's coming from. We both hail from third world countries. We both came to America seeking shelter. We both arrived as poor immigrants hoping for a haven. Now that Mr. Graduate has a chance to attain a better life, how can anyone rightfully deny him that fortuitous opportunity?

Mr. Graduate getting that $1,200,000 paycheck is like getting the winning lottery ticket. Who in their right mind would turn down the winning lottery ticket? I know I wouldn't. And if someone were to brand me as greedy for accepting a million dollar prize, I would say go ahead. I would also say that while they're slapping that label on me, I would proceed to do a lot of good for my family with my fortified bank account. For starters, I would make certain my family never sat down to a paltry supper table again.

Unless I'm way off track in my assessment of Mr. Graduate, he grew up too aware of his family's poverty and longed to provide for his single mother who likely had to go without. Now that he has the opportunity to take care of her, he should definitely seize the opportunity. He should earn as much as he can, while he can. He should secure a sure deal so that his mother will never have to grow another coffee bean to sell for pennies of profit.

If Mr. Graduate were to follow the path of the conventional thinkers, he would go to class and sit at a desk for four years, earn a degree, *then* begin his professional basketball career that will have nothing to do with the degree he spent four years getting. (Michael Jordan got his degree in Geography. Do you think that degree did anything to help him cut through a myriad of defenders and slam the ball into the basket?) And if Mr. Graduate were to go ahead and spend four years getting a college degree merely to have a safety net in case something went wrong with his professional career, what would he lose out on? All things being equal, Mr. Graduate would forego $1,200,000 per year – which means at the end of four years, he would lose out on $4,800,000. Is there any realistic college degree that would earn him $4,800,000 in four years? There are lots of people who will work their entire lives and not come close to earning $4,800,000. What right does any of us have telling Mr. Graduate to pass up the chance to earn $4,800,000 in only four years?

Let's say that young Mr. Graduate ignores the advice of the conventional thinkers and the worst of the naysayers' warnings comes true. Let's say that two years into his pro career, Mr. Graduates suffers severe damage to his anterior crucial ligament ("ACL") and has to hang up his basketball shoes for good. What are his options then? The answer is simple: Mr. Graduate goes to college, sits at a desk for four years, and earns a college degree.

Think about it. If both paths lead to him sitting at a college desk for four years, what difference does it make if he sits at that desk with a bad knee or a good knee? What difference does it make if he sits at that desk before or after a career in professional sports?

Oh, wait. There is a difference, and a very significant one at that.

Even in this worst case scenario, Mr. Graduate would still come out ahead. Proceeding with the same parameters, Mr. Graduate would have invested two years in his professional career. As his reward, he would have $2,400,000 in his bank account (before applicable taxes and deductions, of course). That means he would be starting college $2,400,000 richer than his student peers, the same peers who would most likely be working part-time jobs and earning minimum wage to help pay for their college tuition. Who would be in a better position then? Mr. Graduate who's already a millionaire twice over, or his peers who are making ends meet by working minimum wage jobs? The answer is readily apparent.

Furthermore, if you really want to apply some real-world terms to this worst case scenario, if Mr. Graduate is already a multi-millionaire at the time of his injury, would he really need a college degree? Would he really need a certificate that wouldn't do much more than earn him a conventional income of $40,000 per year? Whip out a calculator and you'll see that a college peer of Mr. Graduate's making $40K a year would have to work 30 years − almost all of their adult life − to earn what Mr. Graduate made in one year.

Some may insist that going to college will do more for Mr. Graduate than give him a good education. They'll say that playing college hoops for four years will hone his basketball skills which, in turn, will make him a better player when he joins a professional team.

This is true.

It's also true that playing for four years on a professional team will hone his skills even more than spending that same amount of time on a college team.

After all, who's better: college players or professional players? (Hint: people will cough up a lot more money to attend an NBA Finals game than they will a collegiate finals game.)

Given the answer to that question, who can provide better, stronger competition: college players or professional players?

Given the answer to that question, who can better hone Mr. Graduate's hoops skills?

Given the answer to that question, it's more than obvious as to where Mr. Graduate should spend his four years after high school.

There is yet another reason why Mr. Graduate should skip college and jump straight into professional sports, and that reason has to do with the outside chance of him having a freak accident on the basketball court. Although the possibility is slim that Mr. Graduate will suffer something so catastrophic, there is a possibility nonetheless. To see real evidence of this, one has to look no further than an incident that occurred around the time of Mr. Graduate's exit from high school.

The annual collegiate NCAA tournament had begun. Sadly, for this season, March Madness virtually took on a literal meaning for a player from Louisville. This particular player had jumped up to block a shot. His upward trajectory was normal. His hard landing was not, for when he came down – his shin bone snapped in half!

The gruesome break drew gasps of horror from the bystanders. The coaches and players standing on the sidelines saw up close the sight of exposed bone and torn, bloody muscle. The ghastly visage left some of them in tears.

Although this player was promptly tended to, and he healed as well as could be expected, his competitive playing days were over.

If this player had been Mr. Graduate who had listened to conventional wisdom and gone to college first only to snap his shin bone in half, his dream of financially providing for his family would have been shattered along with his leg. Professional sports is a business, and no business in its right mind would hire an employee who can't produce. (A cold, hard truth – but a truth nonetheless.) Instead of earning $1,200,000 for one year of his time on a basketball court, Mr. Graduate would have earned $0.

What then?

Would the people who had told Mr. Graduate to put college before a paycheck have dug into their pockets and come up with $1,200,000 as back-up compensation?

No, of course they wouldn't.

They would have offered him their sympathy – a gesture that, while kind in sentiment, is worthless when it comes to obtaining the material needs necessary for a decent life.

Furthermore, a life-altering injury doesn't have to come on the basketball court either. It could come as a freak accident in everyday life. This happens to be something I also know about.

While I was standing on a street corner one sunny afternoon in downtown Los Angeles waiting to cross the street, a speeding car in front of me ran a red light, smashed into the car that had the green light. The next thing I knew, one of the cars went flying onto the sidewalk – straight to where I was standing!

Luckily, I was able to scramble and get out the way. If I hadn't, I could have been seriously hurt – if not killed on the spot – by that runaway car. Who's to say such an accident couldn't happen to Mr. Graduate?

The detractors might say these kinds of accidents are one in a million, and they're probably right. But my rebuttal would be to state that when there is so much at stake, why take that one in a million chance? Why not play it safe and take the path where the risk is zero in a million?

Just in case you think that I'm always emphasizing sports over education, rest assured that I'm not. Due to the teachings of my parents and my cultural background, I will always advocate education and a furtherance of one's knowledge. I'm fully aware that the advancements in a person's schooling will contribute greatly to the advancements in a person's life. With that in mind, I also keep an eye on the big picture: *The advancements in a person's quality of life.*

And that advancement can come in more ways than one.

If this scenario revolved around a person who excelled in cerebral capabilities instead of physical prowess, my advocacy would be the same. I would encourage that person to use his mental mettle to gain as much money as he could, as quickly as he could. If the central figure was Albert Einstein who stood to gain $1,200,000 for flexing his equation of $E=MC^2$ right out of high school, I would also advocate that Mr. Einstein immediately seize his opportunity to gain a big payday. I would say to good old Albert, "You most certainly should seize that lottery-size paycheck and put it to good use. You should buy a nice house for your mother. While you're at it, you should use that money to provide for the long term care of yourself too. Who knows what might happen if you run off to a university and get a degree that you might never use? If you chose that path, you could be walking to class, trip and hit your head on the sidewalk, and suddenly have trouble comprehending that $2 + 2 = 4$. In light of that possibility – no matter how remote – don't even think about going to college first. You grab that $1,200,000 paycheck while you can, and if misfortune catches you and renders you ordinary like the rest of us, you can always go to college at a later date and sit at a desk with the rest of us mortals."

Many will say that a person so young getting so much money will be greatly vulnerable to the pitfalls of wealth. In this regard, I completely agree. That's why I would require that any professional team recruiting a teenager right out of high school provide mandatory, comprehensive financial guidance. This supervision would help not only the player but the team as well. I'm sure that the team's management realizes that any off-court monetary distractions could significantly affect their player's on-court performance. All of this, however, is an entirely different paradigm altogether. Before the prodigy can turn his attention to managing newfound wealth, he must first acquire that newfound wealth, and that can only happen if he signs on the dotted line ASAP.

So there you have it. I'm not biased when it comes to any skill or talent that stands to reap someone a large financial gain. Whether you're good at athletics, scholastics, spouting out rapturous songs with a captivating voice, or twiddling your thumbs – if financial security is within your reach, seize it.

As you may well know, Mr. Graduate isn't the first athlete to skip college and go straight into professional sports. I'm sure you can name a few others, such as a certain Mr. Lebron James who has more than made a mark for himself in the NBA. Since graduating from high school and not wasting any time before cavorting with the Cleveland Cavaliers, he has amassed a fortune so stratospheric that he makes Mr. Graduate look like one of us common folk. That's why I purposely did not want to highlight Mr. James as an example. I didn't want to go into the extremes. I wanted to focus on someone else whose professional paycheck was more conservative – at least as far as professional sports are concerned – so that I could better illustrate my point. As you can see, even with a pay rate as conservative as Mr. Graduate's, it's still better to buck conventional wisdom and bank the financial rewards as soon as possible.

Am I being too capitalistic? Nope. I'm simply being pragmatic. Money is an absolute necessity in life. In case you disagree, I can introduce you to some relatives of mine who make a few dollars a day in the third-world country where I was born. They can tell you how they yearn to earn enough money in order to gain some earthly goods – not to indulge in materialism, mind you – just enough to live a decent life. It's partly through their eyes that I'm encouraging high school graduates like Mr. Graduate to hold off on college and immediately accept the highest contract that comes their way.

Instead of telling these young athletes that they should go to college first so they can have something to fall back on in case something goes wrong with their professional sports career, society should engage in neutral thinking and tell these athletes to leap into professional sports first so they can have something to fall back on in case something goes wrong with their college career.

A Buddhist Thought

If you are a good practitioner, you can easily handle your difficulties. The transformation is quicker. There are many kinds of feelings: painful feelings, pleasant feelings, and neutral feelings. In the process of practicing, we discover that the neutral feelings are very interesting. As when we sit, there is a sensation that is neutral. When we bring mindfulness to the neutral feeling, you find that it is quite nice. You see that you already have enough conditions for happiness with a neutral feeling. If you look deeply at the neutral feeling, you see that it is wonderful. When you see your feelings passing by like a river, you see that [the vast majority] of your neutral feelings are quite pleasant. With mindfulness, our neutral feeling is transformed into happiness.

This is just a little something that I came up with during my lunch break. Yeah, right! If you believe that, there's some great oceanfront property I'd like to sell you in Kansas.

I wish I could dream up something as insightful as this thought during my lunch break, or any other time for that matter. In truth, this astute perception came from Thích Nhất Hạnh, a well-regarded Vietnamese Buddhist monk. As you can see, he encourages a sense of neutral thinking that can create a calm state of mind which in turn can produce wisdom, equanimity, and happiness.

On The Job Sight

We live and learn while we learn to live. I've learned quite a bit about the benefits of neutral thinking from the sights I've seen on the job. What is my job, you might ask? What do I do for a living in order to feed my piggy bank so its stomach won't growl from hunger? Could it be that I'm a prolific writer who lives luxuriously from the bountiful royalties of my books? (Oh, how I wish!) No, my bread-and-butter job is being a flight attendant. (Yeah, yeah, some people don't consider that to be a real job, but that's another story altogether.) For the time being, let's assume it's a real job because in my eyes, any job that pays real money is a real job. Also for the time being, rest assured that I've learned quite a bit from the sights I've seen on the job.

•

It's no secret that when you work with the public, you run into some oddball situations. The veracity of that statement is even truer when you work with the public who are confined in a metallic tube speeding through the air at 400 miles per hour.

Although I've been "walking on air" (my terminology for choosing to have an airborne workplace) for almost two decades, a story that remains prominent in my mind is one that took place when I'd been on the job for only a few weeks. Back then, it was still customary for the airlines to serve a complimentary meal, and on this particular evening flight, I was setting up the carts in the back of the plane for the dinner service when I heard the "ding" of a call button. I walked up to where the call light was lit and asked the couple sitting there if I could be of service to them.

Right away, an obese woman in the aisle seat spoke up and said, "Yes, there's something wrong with my tray table."

13

"Oh?" I replied. "What's wrong with it?"

The woman with the large, protruding stomach declared, "My tray table won't come all the way down."

Puzzled, I said, "It won't?"

"No," she stated as she reached out and turned the fastener that held the tray table in place. The tray table came down – halfway – and hit her protruding stomach. "See?" she said, pointing to the tray table with an air of vindication. "It won't come all the way down. What's wrong with it?"

I looked at her in disbelief, inadvertently doing a terrific impression of a deer caught in headlights. Wasn't it obvious why the tray table won't come down all the way? Couldn't she see that it was her big, protruding stomach that was in the way? Didn't she know that the answer to her own question was monumentally evident?

A couple of seconds casually sauntered by as I looked at her while she quizzically looked back at me. I was hoping that she would come to her senses and take back her bizarre inquiry. I was even praying that she would abruptly say, "Ha, ha! I was playing a joke on you! Got you good, didn't I?" But alas, none of that happened. My hope and prayer went unanswered as I continued to look at her while she continued to stare back at me. "Um . . . uh . . . um," I could only mumble with definite indecision as I tried to buy some time to formulate a diplomatic reply.

As my poor luck would have it, while I was trying to buy that time, the matter got worse. Before I knew it, the woman reached over to her husband's tray table and said, "His tray table works just fine. What's wrong with mine?" And again, to demonstrate her point, she turned the fastener holding up her spouse's tray table, lowered it completely, and said in a justified tone of voice: "See? How come my tray table can't do that?"

My eyes went straight to the stomach of the man sitting next to her. It as a stomach that wasn't big. It wasn't obstinate, and it certainly wasn't protruding. If anything, it was a stomach that was on the skinny side. My sight traveled upwards to meet his gaze, and the dumbfounded expression on my face must have been flashing the question: *Do you know why your wife is asking me this bizarre question?* – because he promptly shrugged his shoulders to answer: *I don't know what to tell you.*

Since I was left to my own devices, and since I didn't know what to say, I lamely muttered to the woman, "Maybe . . . the tray table . . . is . . . broken?" Although I knew this wasn't the best of answers, I also knew it wasn't the worst of answers either because at least I had avoided spitting out: "The tray table won't come down all the way because your big, fat stomach is in the way!"

Without any hesitation, my oversized passenger seized upon the premise I presented and began to tell me how she wanted me to proceed once I began the meal service. "In that case," she stated, "when you serve me my dinner, don't bring me the whole tray at once."

Perplexed, I asked her, "Don't bring you the whole tray at once?"

"That's right. Since my tray table is broken, I don't have any place to put my tray. Don't bring me the whole tray all at once. Bring it to me one piece at a time."

No less perplexed, I asked her: "Bring the tray to you one piece at a time?"

"Yes, bring me the salad first, then when I'm done with that, you can bring me the entrée. After that, you can bring me the dessert. You know what I mean, right?"

Oh, she wanted me to bring her the individual containers on the tray one piece at a time. I nodded in comprehension while recognizing that the more I prolonged this dialogue, the more I was allowing her the chance to throw another oddball request at me. To prevent that from happening, I simply stated, "I'll see what I can do," – and hurriedly scurried away to the back of the plane.

As I was making my escape, a funny thing happened. Just I started to run away like the scared rabbit that I was, I passed by a lady who was sitting two rows behind the portly passenger, on the other side of the aisle. I noticed she was regarding me with a broad smile – so broad that she seemed to be suppressing a burst of laughter. It dawned on me that she had witnessed the entire exchange and was amused by what she saw and heard. Seeing that she was amused made me amused, and that amusement leaped ten-fold after I heard what she had to say. When she crooked a finger at me, telling me to come closer, I did. As soon as I leaned forward, she whispered in my ear, "You poor thing!"

Suddenly, I felt my own burst of laughter ready to jump out of me. In case I couldn't contain it, I didn't want to be in the presence of the big woman for fear of offending her. Hurriedly, I went to the back of the plane where a gigantic guffaw *did* leap out of me.

What does all this have to do with neutral thinking? The lesson I learned was that just because someone else is going to the extremes doesn't mean I have to as well.

Later on, when I reflected on the episode, I think the obese woman was embarrassed of her size and tried to get around it by posing an odd request. Due to the awkwardness of the situation, she inadvertently went into the extremes by asking me why the tray table won't come all the way down. In hindsight, I'm glad I didn't join her in going off the deep end. I'm glad I stayed in a neutral territory and avoided making the situation any worse.

Oh . . . I forgot to tell you how the story ended. As happenstance would have it, a few minutes after I scurried to the back of the plane, the captain came on the P.A. and said that the aircraft had developed a mechanical issue and the flight was cancelled. All the passengers grabbed their bags, got off the plane, and went on another flight. As a result, there was no dinner service, and I never saw that woman again.

Fence Sitters Wanted

Too often, the term "fence sitter" gets saddled with a negative connotation. It brings to mind someone who's in the middle, someone who doesn't act right away to conclusively plant their flag on one side of the issue or the other. Too often, this term is completely undeserving of its undesirable connotation.

How so?

Before we proceed to that answer, let's get an unbiased definition first.

The dictionary defines a "fence sitter" as "One who takes neither side in a controversy, but maintains a neutral position."

In short, a fence sitter is someone who's neutral. Is that really so bad?

Why can't being a fence sitter be perceived as something good? Why can't being neutral be interpreted as something positive?

If you stop and think about it, not only can being neutral be rewarding, but in some ways, it's absolutely necessary.

•

The United States Of America is a wonderful country to claim as the nation of your home for many reasons, one of which is a court system that embraces due process. If you're accused of a crime, you're innocent until proven guilty – not the other way around. Depending on the nature of your case, it may be a jury (as opposed to a judge) who decides your outcome. Before, during, and even after the argument of your case, what does the court tell the jury to do?

You guessed it.

Be neutral.

The court, in its effort to bring forth fairness for all, specifies that the jury is to consider the presented facts only and nothing else. It tells the jury not to take sides. It directs the jury to maintain a neutral point of view. In essence, the court tells the jury to be a fence sitter.

In the rare chance that you still disagree with this depiction, feel free to go to a country that doesn't endorse a system of due process, one that doesn't strive for fairness. Get yourself accused of a crime, have the finger pointed at you as an alleged perpetrator, and you'll likely see how fast the word "alleged" disappears. More likely than not, you'll find yourself looking down the barrel of a gun disguised as a system that has tossed aside the laughable premise of innocent until proven guilty. Once you've dug yourself into that hole, you'll find yourself wishing for a fence sitter, a jury who will look upon your case with a neutral frame of mind.

~

It's not only the jury that's told to be a fence sitter in the court system. It's also the judge. Consider a civil matter such as a divorce. Two adults who once professed eternal love for one another are now locked in a dispute so bitter that it makes a drop of grapefruit juice taste sweeter than a glass of orange soda. Worse, the couple has a child, and both ex-spouses are arming themselves for a rancorous war to win them custody of that child.

And it's up to the judge to make sure the kid comes out of it in one piece.

How should the judge go about this? Should she immediately take a side? Should she immediately favor the mother because society tends to see women as more nurturing? Should she immediately favor the father because society tends to see men as better wage earners? Should she automatically subscribe to one of those traditional perceptions, or should she step back and approach the matter with an untethered, objective mindset?

Maybe the mother in this particular case isn't as nurturing as society would portray her. Maybe the father makes less money than the mother but is much more attentive towards his child than his ex-wife could ever be. Maybe neither parent comes close to being a good guardian and the child shouldn't stay with either one of them.

Common sense dictates that the judge must consider the crucial facets of a particular case and do what's best for the child. In order to do that, she must be a fence sitter. She must be neutral in deliberating all the details so she can arrive at the best life-outcome for the creation of the once blissful union.

~

Working alongside the court system is the long arm of the law, and the reach of that appendage must also remain neutral while serving and protecting the public. When the police get a call to handle a domestic dispute, for example, they can't show up on the scene and jump to conclusions. They can't immediately favor one side over the other. Upon arrival, they have to be a fence sitter and gather the facts from all parties. Once they have those facts, then they can act accordingly. In the meantime, they have to stay neutral.

I have an acquaintance who, unfortunately, knows this all too well. "Ted" and his wife are going through an acrimonious divorce. They have two kids. To make a long (and very convoluted) story short, suffice to say that Ted must continue to reside in the house while he divorces his wife.

One evening, Ted gave his son a playful pinch. His wife immediately called the police and told them her husband was abusing their son. Two policemen came to the house right away. If these officers had been the kind to jump to conclusions, they would have arrested Ted then and there. Instead, they did their job correctly. They approached the matter objectively. They stayed neutral while they gathered the facts – including noting the report that the wife was alone in her house weeks earlier and started screaming so loudly that the neighbors called the police who arrived only to find that there was reason for the wife to be screaming so loudly.

Once the police had the facts regarding Ted's playful pinch, they couldn't find any reason to take him into custody. So they simply excused themselves from the house while taking note that the wife, in addition to screaming with alarm for no valid reason, had called the police to her house because of a playful pinch.

~

And you know who else makes a good fence sitter? An effective referee. Whether it's a football game, a boxing match, or a basketball game, there is so much money at stake in professional sports these days that it is absolutely critical to have an unbiased person in the game who knows how to keep it clean and true. Not only are referees needed to call the fouls they see, they're also needed to *not* call the fouls they don't see.

Yes, you read that right. Referees are needed in the game to make "non-calls."

If that sounds strange to you, tune into an NBA game, and you're bound to see two opposing players bumping into one another as they compete for a particular spot on the court. Sometimes, one of the players will suddenly fall to the floor as if he'd been blatantly fouled, performing a "flop" in order to persuade the referee to call a foul against his opponent. If the referee is easily manipulated, he may fall for the trick and proceed to make that false call. But if he is an effective referee, he will see the flop for what is — a fake foul — and ignore it, thereby making a good non-call.

Making a non-call is a lot like performing a non-action. Sometimes, it's best to remain neutral and do nothing. While you mull that over, please note that I said "non-action" — not "inaction."

There is a difference.

"Inaction" is not doing something when you should be. If there's a fire, you should definitely be doing something. You should definitely grab the nearest fire extinguisher to put out the fire, or call 9-1-1, or act in some way to address the emergency. To do nothing would undeniably make you culpable of inaction.

"Non-action" is not doing something because it's the best course of action. This notion hit home with me when I was watching the game show *The Family Feud*. One of the questions posed to the contestants in effect asked: "What's the best thing to do when someone is yelling at you?" To my surprise, one gentleman answered, "Nothing." The more I thought about it, the more I realized how true the answer was, especially when it comes to life in the big city.

Without realizing it, I have practiced that gentleman's answer quite a few times while walking down the crowded streets of cities like Los Angeles, Chicago, and New York City. Mixed into the hustle and bustle of these teeming cities are quite a few homeless people, some of whom aren't the most rational people you'll ever meet. It's not uncommon to come upon a homeless person who will yell at you for no apparent reason, and if you're loony enough to yell back at them, you might make the matter worse, much worse. Not only are some of these homeless folks ragged and dirty, a few of them are also deranged. In addition to yelling at you for no good reason, one or two of them are liable to hit you, or come at you with a weapon!

So what's the best thing for you to do in response? Like the gentleman said on *The Family Feud* – nothing.

Keep your wits about you, don't say anything, and keep walking. Simply put, be a fence sitter and do nothing.

~

Road Rage.

We've all heard about it. Some of us have seen it. A few of us have probably experienced it.

Once, I saw it twice, both in a span of 10 minutes within a 1 mile stretch of road.

It was during rush hour in the vicinity of Los Angeles City College. As the north bound traffic on that multi-lane boulevard was inching along painfully slow, a lot of people's frustration was spiking painfully fast.

The first incident flared up when one guy cut off another guy. The second incident erupted when two women shouted an insult at another woman. In both occurrences, fists went flying. Thankfully, a gun never appeared. Fortunately, no bullets went flying.

Regrettably, that wasn't the case with some other incidents that made it into the news – one of which concerned a teenager named Trayvon Martin and a man named George Zimmerman. After the jury had rendered its verdict of that trial, one of the jurors tearfully said she wished the confrontation never happened. She said she wished that both of them had walked away, that the tragedy had never happened.

I've heard other people who have been in confrontations with serious fallouts say the same thing afterwards. Practically all of them say they wish they could have given themselves a sort of time-out before the escalation got out of hand. If they had, they would have gotten a chance to put matters into perspective. They would have seen that the consequences just weren't worth the altercation, and they would have given themselves the chance to simply walk away.

In other words, they wish they could have been a fence sitter so they could pause, and do nothing, while rationalizing the merits of the matter.

That way, they could have stepped back and stayed on the right side of the fence instead of falling over and ending up on the wrong side of the fence.

Hindsight makes for great foresight. That's why I hope to make other people's hindsight my foresight. It's good to learn from your mistakes. It's even better to learn from other people's irreversible errors.

The next time someone cuts me off in traffic, I'll remind myself to be a fence sitter. I'll give myself a sort of time-out to think things over. I'll remind myself that there are people who depend on me, namely an elderly mother who doesn't get around too well. I'll refrain from succumbing to road rage because nothing good will come out of it. If I severely harm the other person and "win" the fight, I could still lose because I'll probably end up in prison for a very long time. Who will help my mother get around then? If the other person significantly harms me, I would lose for sure, maybe as badly as being the guest of honor at my own funeral. Who will help my mother get around then? Either way, it would be a lose/lose situation. Who in their right mind would want to enter a contest where they'll lose for sure?

Not me, so before I give in to a road rage, I hope to pause, do nothing, and give myself time to brush off the encounter as a mere ruffle. I'll allow the occurrence to ruffle my feathers, but then I'll collect myself and move on. With some providence, I'll head off road rage at the pass and take the exit towards a road ruffle.

~

I'll bet most of you are fence sitters when it comes to politics. The vast majority of people are moderates, and the moderates are the people who place themselves in the middle of the political spectrum. That naturally makes them fence sitters.

I should know because I'm a moderate myself.

We moderates don't jump off the diving board and go flailing into the waters of the far right or the far left. On the contrary, we stay centered in our perspectives. We try to be even-tempered in our political outlook.

George Washington and his fellow Founding Fathers must have been moderates too because that's how they set up the government of this nation. They strived to build a system that was well-balanced, one that didn't go diving headfirst into the extremes.

Having won the war for independence from the British, they could have replicated the monarchy already established in the mother country. Instead, they purposefully steered clear of that set up. They avoided any scheme that bestowed all the power in one person and established a government that divided the power into three different groups: The Executive Branch (President), The Legislative Branch (Congress), and The Judicial Branch (Supreme Court). They founded a Checks and Balances system that allowed each branch to keep tabs on the other branches. They provided a means for each branch to have a say in the matters of the total government. They took precautions to prevent any one person or group of persons from seizing all the power.

Some may argue that it's better to find a person who's virtuous and let that person take control of the whole country. While espousing a benevolent dictatorship may sound wise and it might have a chance in a fantasy world, it is destined to fail in the real world. Several scenarios would assuredly surface, none of them good.

A kindly despot may become corrupted by power, and once he does, there's nothing to stop him from abusing his complete authority.

A virtuous ruler may stay true to the ideal of benevolence but unexpectedly be felled by an assassin's bullet. Once she's dead, who's to stop another person who isn't so benevolent from assuming power and abusing that all-encompassing power?

An altruistic king may be able to avoid both the temptation of power and the assassin's bullet, but he will always be prone to human error. None of us are perfect. All of us make mistakes. None of us hits a home run every time we step up to the plate. All of us are bound to strike out once in a while. What it the ruler at bat strikes out monumentally in his judgement of a gargantuan decision. (Think nuclear missiles and red "the button.") If no one can correct him, he might inflict devastating damage upon the masses with his good intentions. Where would the well-being of the public be then?

All in all, bestowing absolute power in one person just isn't feasible in the real world. Fairly spreading the supremacy is the only workable solution. It may not be an ideal solution, but it is the best solution given all our human foibles. That's why the Founding Fathers wanted to ensure that America's government was evenly divided. They knew that power can destroy just as it can construct. They recognized that sovereignty is much too precarious to be perched on the pinnacle of a pin. They understood that authority must be set on stable ground. That's why they modified the monarchy and converted the government into a neutral, three-way Checks and Balances system.

~

Infrequently – thanks goodness it's infrequently – I'm amazed at how some people don't see the obvious that's just beneath the ostensible and end up doing something harmful to themselves. An instance that comes to mind was when my friend "Cara" saw an advertisement where a company said they had come up with a great product that stood to make a lot of money, but they didn't want to keep the secret of their product to themselves, so they were willing to share it with others in exchange for a small payment.

Cara, a college graduate and an otherwise smart person who excelled in the field of math and sciences, bought the pitch and was about to send in a payment until I pointed out a fact she should have noticed herself: *If the product was so great and if the company stood to make a lot of money from it, why would they want to share it with others? Why wouldn't they want to keep their secret a secret so they can make a lot of money for themselves?*

Think of the drink Coca-Cola, I suggested. The secret to making Coke isn't public knowledge because the company has kept that secret for themselves. As a result, they have made a lot of money for themselves. I told Cara that the advertisement she saw was tantamount to Coca-Cola telling people that Coca-Cola will reveal their secret in exchange for a small fee. There's no way Coca-Cola would do that because the small fee they would receive would be pennies compared to the vast fortune they've made for themselves – and will keep making for themselves because they never shared their secret with anybody.

Cara saw my neutral perspective. She paused, became a fence sitter, and grasped that the real product touted in the advertisement she saw was trickery. Needless to say, she didn't that company a single dime.

~

For the past decade, I've been hearing more and more about the trouble that Social Security is in. The more I hear about it, the more I began to worry that Social Security might not be around when I retire, or that if it is still around, it'll be so decrepit that it'll be hobbling along just like me in my old age. That's why I've been bolstering my personal retirement accounts as much as I can.

When I did my research into the different mutual funds that are available for my Roth IRA, I kept running into funds that said "No Load" – giving average investors like me the impression that the financial company doesn't charge a fee to administer that fund. When I first saw these "No Load" declarations, I thought: *Awesome! They don't charge a fee for their services. That'll save me money!*

And then I stopped and thought about it some more. If these financial companies don't charge a fee, that means they don't make any money. If they don't make any money, that means they don't get a paycheck. If they don't get a paycheck, that means they're working for . . . free?

That didn't make any sense, so I called them up to get to the bottom of the matter. The Customer Representative who answered my call offered me a reply that was far from exact. Actually, his reply was so long-winded, off-topic, and meandering that I got tired of politely listening to him and said, "Look, this No Load thing makes me think you're working for free, and I know that can't be true. If you don't make any money, then how do you stay in business? Since you are in business, and since you're staying in business, that means you're making money – which is fine with me because I don't expect you to work for free. Just tell me how you make that money so we can both be upfront about it."

After a short silence, the company representative finally gave me the answer I was looking for. He told me to go into the section where it discusses the mutual fund's "Expense Ratio." He said that's the fee the company charges. He said that fee is how the company makes its money.

Informed, I explored the details of the funds' Expense Ratio. The more I found out about the actual costs, the more I was glad I was able to go into a neutral mode and enable myself to get the answer I needed.

~

As long as I'm back-slapping myself for some favorable financial tactics, I might as well harp on another happenstance that proved to be beneficial to me. When the housing crisis caused a severe economic downturn in 2008, the stock market plummeted faster than a boulder falling off a cliff. A lot of people at my workplace saw their 401(k) savings account sink to a new low. When they thought it couldn't get any lower, the market got even worse, and they saw their life savings sink even lower. Nervous that their retirement account was dwindling down to a decrepit state, some of them stopped making monthly contributions to their account altogether.

I wasn't above the fray myself.

I also saw a large sum of money disappearing from my retirement account. I was contemplating taking the same actions my colleagues were taking, all the while wondering: *Should I stop contributing to my 401(k)? If I don't, there's a good chance I'll be putting money into my account only to see it disappear. Should I go a step further? Should I withdraw some money before it does down the drain like some of the companies that have gone down the drain in this crisis?*

Despite the fact that I was seeing the money I'd put away for many years evaporate like a wet sponge set out beneath a scorching sun, I did keep in mind some tried and true facts about economics and investing:

- Steady contributions over time will yield favorable results.
- Buy low, sell high.
- Just about everything that goes down, including the stock market, will come back up – and when it does, it's best to have bought the stocks at a low price – which means I need to keep making monthly contributions so I can buy the stocks at a low price.
- Don't give in to emotions. The fear in those emotions may force an investor to sell when the prices are low, only to buy back those same stocks at a later date when the prices are high.

As hard as it was, I kept all that in mind as I committed myself to being a financial fence sitter. Once I did, I succeeded in performing a difficult task in a time of turmoil: *I did nothing.*

I didn't reduce my monthly contributions to my 401(k), and I certainly didn't withdraw any money. (Even an average investor like me knew about the penalties for an early withdrawal.) Moreover, I applied the same resolution towards my Roth IRA. I kept up the same contributions I'd made for years and didn't withdraw anything.

I'd be more than fibbing if I said I never thought about changing my mind. About once a week, I would check the amount set aside for when I'm old and gray, and it was disheartening to see myself getting poorer and poorer by the week. Visions of me enjoying a plate of spaghetti and meatballs in my rocking chair were disintegrating into a vision of me slurping on a styrofoam cup of ramen instant noodles. Nevertheless, I maintained the course, and my adherence to the counsel of those much wiser than me eventually reaped rich rewards.

Gradually, the economy improved. Very slowly at first, then by heartening leaps and plentiful bounds, my retirement account packed on the pounds it had lost during its financial fasting. Prior to the economic downturn, I had been actively contributing to my 401(k) for about 10 years, maximizing it whenever possible. Once the economy took an upturn, it took me only 5 years to double the amount I had accumulated in 10 years. Yep, twice the money in half the time.

Thankfully, if I'm slurping on a cup of ramen noodles in my old age, it'll be because I'm too lazy to get out of my rocking chair to whip up a batch of spaghetti and meatballs that I can easily afford.

~

Financial turmoil is one thing. The turmoil from the death of a loved one is an entirely different matter.

While on the 3rd draft of this book, I attended my 30th high school reunion. I was driving to the gathering with a friend of mine when I mentioned the book's theme to him. At first, he was perplexed by the "neutral" idea of it. When I said that part of being neutral is to do nothing, especially when heightened emotions are involved, he immediately understood the concept and related an applicable instance.

His wife's mother died unexpectedly a few years earlier. When she passed away, a lot of his father-in-law's friends gave him a note of advice along with their condolences. They told him not to make any big decisions for about another year. Whether the decision had to do with a significant matter like selling a car, or moving to another house, or changing to a different job, they said to wait. His grief was too great, they counseled, to allow him to make a sound decision. He needed to heal, and to heal, he needed to wait.

The widower heeded their advice. In hindsight, he was very glad he did. He avoided making any big decisions that could have resulted in monumental mistakes. He coped well. He healed well. He felt blessed that he did nothing.

~

There was a time in my life when I wished I had done nothing. After fleeing Vietnam and settling down in Kansas as a kid, I started school not knowing any English. I wanted badly to jump into the mainstream of school matters and immediately integrate myself into the classroom. Of course, that was impossible. Learning a brand new language takes time, lots of time. The kid that I was back then should have known that, but I was too ignorant to know any better. As a consequence, I tried to do too much, too fast, and threw myself into the self-dug pit of despair and frustration.

If the adult version of me could have talked to the kid version of me then, I would have said, "Slow down, way down. There's nothing you can do about your complete lack of English. To think that you can immediately overcome that immovable obstacle would be to think that you can pick up a two-ton boulder, lift it over your head, and heave it a thousand yards. It's not realistic, and it's not gonna happen. Just sit still, do nothing, and take your time absorbing all the new sights and sounds all around you. While you may not realize it, doing nothing right now will do you a lot of good!"

Fast forward about 25 years, I'm an adult and the 2.0 version of me has learned well the mistakes of the 1.0 version of me. I know when I've come upon an obstacle I cannot budge. I know not to dig myself a pit of despair because I'm not able to heave a two-ton boulder a thousand yards. I'm very cognizant that the wisest course of action can be to do nothing at all.

The revised version of me is in a restaurant in Germany, and I needed to use the restroom. After stepping away from the table and going the allocated spot for the restrooms, I got a surprise. The words for "Men" and "Women" on the restroom doors were in German. I can't read German, so I looked for the pictures that specify the genders, such as a man wear a suit or a woman wearing a dress. To my dismay, there were no such pictures. Not wanting to walk in the wrong door and hearing a loud shriek to go along with the German version of: "Get out, you pervert!" – I was at a loss as to what to do.

Then I took the advice I would have given to my younger self: *Do nothing.*

I decided to stand outside the doors and see who came out of which restroom. If I saw a guy coming out of a certain door, I knew that was the door for me. If I saw a woman coming out of a particular door, I knew that wasn't the door for me. After hanging out for a couple of minutes, I saw a guy came waltzing out of the door to my left, letting me know which restroom was right for me. I went in there, made use of the facilities, relieved I was able to reap the rewards of doing nothing.

~

Can we jump back to the "No Loads" topic for a second? Thinking about that made think of something else.

When I first started my job and began flying to foreign countries, I often saw money exchange places that said: "No fees." Without really thinking about it, I thought that these places were being altruistic somehow by not charging a fee for their services. But then I took off my dunce cap for a minute and realized how my assumption didn't make any sense. I began asking myself some basic questions. If these money exchange places didn't charge a fee, that means they didn't make any money. If they didn't make any money, how did they pay their bills? If they couldn't pay their bills due to not having any money, how could they stay in business? If they couldn't stay in business, how could they maintain a shop, especially one that didn't charge a fee?

Just as importantly, they're a business, not a charitable nonprofit organization. Surely, they're not going through the trouble of exchanging money for us travelers out of the goodness of their heart. Surely, they're making a profit

31

somehow. If so, that's fine with me. I just wish they would be honest about it.

I never bothered to ask the people working at these shops how they could stay in business if they charged "No fees." I suspected that if they're dodgy enough to proclaim they charged "No fees," then they're elusive enough to avoid any inquiries about the sanctity of their business scheme. My guess is that they somehow inserted a profit mechanism into their money exchanges and hoped no one would think to look beyond their "No fees" proclamation.

~

In my travels, on and off the job, I've come across a couple of examples that illustrate the benefits of neutral thinking. As you'll see, "Gracias, Barcelona *Policia*" and "Gracias, Barcelona Bystanders" exemplify how seeking the aid of a fence sitter can have positive results, and how a certain "Captain Cuckoo" exemplifies that *not* being a fence sitter can prohibit the benefits of neutral thinking.

Gracias, Barcelona *Policia*

I had never stayed in a hostel before, and that was why I committed a cardinal sin when it came to booking a hostel room. Instead of booking a bed for one night and giving myself an opportunity to see what the hostel was really like once I got there, I reserved – and paid for – a bed for multiple nights based on the photos displayed on the hostel's website. (Please don't get out the wet noodle to whip me just yet. There are more reasons to come for that.)

It happened around 2003. I'd never been to Spain before and thought I'd pay that country a visit. From what I read in the guide books, Barcelona seemed like a good introduction to the country. There was the Gaudi Museum to see. There was the famous *Las Ramblas* area to check out. There was also the Pablo Picasso Museum. (There's more to come on that fiasco.)

A regular hotel room was beyond my budget, so I chose to go with a hostel – an accommodations arrangement that wasn't unlike a big dorm room filled with multiple beds along with a community bathroom. I went online and found a bunch of them. The plethora of choices was so overwhelming, in fact, that it took me several days to narrow my options down to one. What was the deciding factor, you ask?

Well, the hostel's description said it was new, and it boasted of a sparking cleanliness – qualities that are hard to beat when it came to picking a good hostel. Days later, after I'd arrived at the hostel, I would discover that the hostel was indeed new and that it lived up to its billing as being clean. The cleanliness was a plus, but it was a plus that paled in comparison to the minuses.

The *Las Ramblas* area was lively, inviting, and swarming with tourists. As I walked through this hub of activity to get to my hostel, I got an upbeat feeling that made my visit seem very promising. And then I reached my hostel. The place was new all right, and the person who did the interior decorating must have been an ex-convict!

Prominently displayed throughout the institution were stark beams of steel and somber tones of stone. The harsh, austere mood of the hostel was so depressing that while a handful of us tourists were sitting around the lobby waiting for our turn to use the computer, one of the guys looked all around him, took in the hostel's alienating interior, and remarked, "I've never been in a prison before, but this must be what it feels like."

The rest of us could only nod in arrested agreement.

Despite the confining facets of the hostel, it didn't enter my mind to vacate the place. Although I wasn't too keen on the hostel's appearance, I didn't come to Barcelona to revel in a hostel's charm. Additionally, there was also the fact that I was going to be sharing my room with five other people. I wasn't thrilled about that either, but from what I'd gleaned on the internet about the other hostels in the area, that was pretty much the going norm. Besides, since I was only going to be in the correctional facility . . . I mean . . . hostel . . . for five nights, and since I was going to spend most of my time out and about anyway, I figured I could overlook the hostel's hostage-taking design.

That afternoon, I went out exploring. I mingled with the massive crowds that rambled about *Las Ramblas*. I marveled at the street performers, particularly a guy who'd transformed himself into a picture-perfect devil. He was seated on his throne. He was coated in red from head to toe. He was brandishing a pair of horns on the top of his head while wielding a pitchfork in his hand, captivating the awed onlookers who had formed a semi-circle around him. As the throng of tourists snapped their pictures and recorded their videos, he simply sat and grinned and sneered at the crowd in good, clean, malicious fun.

After contributing to Satan's can set out for tips, I moved on. I walked past a police station, or "*Policia*" as the sign above the entrance read, and kept meandering before I stumbled upon a *pension* ("pen·see·on"). I'd heard of a *pension* before but had never seen one in person. To cure my curiosity, I went inside and took a look around.

What the official difference was between a hostel and a *pension*, I really couldn't tell you offhand. All I know is that the gem I found was warm and inviting instead of cold and forbidding. Plus, the *pension* arrangement was set up so that each guest had a small room to himself, thereby allowing some privacy – unlike the hostels I'd come across that were basically crowded dorm rooms providing about as much privacy as a dressing room without the four surrounding walls. (Oh . . . so maybe that was the difference between a *pension* and a hostel.)

Anyway, after I inquired with the clerk at the front desk – a balding, older gentleman with a no-nonsense air about him – I learned that the price for a whole room at the *pension* was about the same as a single bed at the hostel.

A whole room to myself versus a single bed in a big dorm room.

Hhmmm. It was time for a decision, and the decision was a no-brainer. I'll take a room to myself over a bed among many others any day of the week. I told the clerk I would be switching my living quarters and would like a room at his place for the next five nights. I knew I would be losing the cost of one night's stay at the prison-like hostel since that was the establishment's cancellation policy, but it would be worth it because I would have a room to myself. That would be the worst of it, I assumed, until I was informed otherwise by the hostel staff.

"What do you mean no?" I asked the plump woman behind the counter once I'd returned to the hostel and told them of my change in plans.

"No, we cannot refund your money," the woman replied irritably.

Maybe she misunderstood me, I postulated. The cancellation policy on their website stated that if I cancelled my reservation, they would keep the cost of the first night's stay. That was fair enough. As long as they returned the remaining four nights to me, I was willing to take my losses and be on my way. Maybe this woman thought that I wanted her to refund the entire five nights' stay.

I tried to clarify the matter with her. "I don't want you to refund me the entire five nights, just the remaining four nights. You can keep the first night's cost."

"No."

I waited for her to say something additional by way of explanation. When I saw there was nothing more forthcoming, I pressed on with my case. "But that's what it says on your website."

Her reply was abrupt as it was prickly: "No! No refund!"

Seconds earlier, I was dumbfounded. Now I was upset. Keeping my rising irritation in check, I started to ask her again why she wasn't giving me my due refund, but I saw that I would have been continuing a vicious circle. It was time to alter my approach. "I would like to talk to your supervisor," I told her.

"Why?"

My reply was abrupt as it was prickly: "Because I said so!"

She fixed a frozen stare on me, most likely trying to get me to back off. When she saw I wasn't going to budge, she went to the back and got her supervisor.

The second woman was just as plump and uncooperative as her underling. When she stepped up to the counter with her cohort behind her, I could tell from her callous expression that I would be getting more of the same treatment. Despite that outlook, I put my best foot forward.

"Hi," I said to her evenly.

"No refund!" she spat out without even a preamble. Apparently, she'd been briefed on the subject was determined to carry on with the unjust decision. Just as apparently, the mood behind the counter had escalated from prickly to combative.

A brick wall was looming in front of me, and I could see I was flying straight at it headfirst. Nevertheless, if I was going to hit it head on, I was going to hit it while trying my hardest. "But your policy said –"

"No!"

I was at a crossroads. Here I was, a tourist in a foreign country. I didn't want to start any trouble. I could simply walk away, cut my losses, and absorb the $120 loss as a lesson well-learned. But I just couldn't bring myself to just walk away. There was a principle at stake. Moreover, the way these two women were talking to me was really goading my gall. If they didn't want to return my money to me, then maybe an arm of the law known as the *Policia* would be of help.

I squared my sights on the supervisor and said, "If you don't give me back my money, I will report you to the police."

Without batting her eye, she shooed me away with her hands and snorted, "Fine. Go to the police."

Resolute, I told her: "I will."

The *"Policia"* sign that I had passed by earlier was inconspicuous. I was afraid I would have trouble finding it again. Luckily, I didn't.

The officer at the front desk exuded an air of toughness that practically blared out the warning: *Don't break the law and I won't break you!* The man was in his fifties and had a head full of salt and pepper hair to go with his square shoulders. As much as I want to say I can recall his name, I can't, so I'll have to refer to him as "Bruno."

As I approached Bruno, I didn't want to do what I've seen so many Americans do in a foreign country – expect a person in that country to speak their language. I have never said – and will never say – to someone in another country in a demanding tone of voice: "HEY, YOU SPEAK ENGLISH?" Instead, I will try to greet them in English with a fully-worded greeting such as: "Hello. How are you today?" That way, not only is it the proper salutation to begin a conversation, but it's also a subtle way to say, "Sorry. I don't speak your language. Can you speak mine?"

"Hello. How are you today?" I offered Bruno.

He looked up from his desk. "Hola," he returned with a minimal effort.

Uh-oh, I thought. That was not a good sign. Somehow, I got the impression that Bruno was tired of English-speaking tourists coming in to the police station and expecting him to accommodate them in their language. I also got the feeling that if I pressed on in English, Bruno was going to become more resistant than accommodating. Be that as it may, I didn't have any choice. As much as I wanted to explain my predicament to him in Spanish, I couldn't. The only Spanish I knew came from a TV advertisement for a popular Mexican restaurant in the States, and I was pretty sure "Yo quiero Taco Bell" wouldn't be quite appropriate.

"Um," I proceeded with hesitation, "hablas Ingles?"

"No, hablas Español?" Bruno returned while giving me a grin that took me a few moments to decipher.

Dandy, I thought with some dejection. I asked him if he spoke English. He said no and asked me if I spoke Spanish. We were not off to a good start. He had a chip on his shoulder all right, but I could see where he was coming from. If I was at my work place in the U.S.A. and some foreigner came in expecting me to speak their language, I might have a chip on my shoulder too.

That said, I have to admit that the man was slightly irritating me. It seemed like he was going out of his way to be unaccommodating. Couldn't he bend a little to help out someone in need, I wondered?

I immigrated to America from Vietnam at a young age. English, for all intents and purposes, had become my native tongue. Nevertheless, I still can speak a smattering of Vietnamese. When Bruno tossed out his ornery "Hablas Español?" – I was tempted to toss back at him, "No, hablas Vietnamese?" – to ask if he spoke Vietnamese. To have done that, of course, would have been to shoot myself in the foot. I needed Bruno's assistance and alienating him would not have been in my best interest.

"No, I don't speak Spanish," I stated, purposely putting a neutral tone in my voice while confirming that if we were to move forward, it would have to be in English. Two things could have happened at this juncture. Bruno could have insisted we converse in Spanish which would have thrown an insurmountable roadblock in front of me, or he could have relented and opened up an avenue for me in English. Fortunately, he chose the latter.

Bruno raised his forefinger and said something that I understood to mean, "One moment, please." He went to the back office and returned with a colleague. This second officer was younger, probably in his late twenties and a couple of decades away from the paunch that Bruno was sporting. (To my regret, I never got the second officer's name either, so for the sake of convenience, I'll have to refer to him with an alias too.)

"Can I help you?" Carlos said.

Relieved that I could speak freely in English, I explained to the younger officer what happened at the hostel. I also asked him if he could accompany me back there to help me get my refund back. Before he answered, he turned to his older counterpart and relayed my account in Spanish. To my gratification, Bruno was nodding his head agreeably as he listened to the translated account. Judging by his body language and his facial expression, I gathered that he seemed to be warming up to my quest for justice.

When Carlos finished his translation, he turned to me and said, "Okay. We go." By "we," I assumed he meant him and me. That's why I was surprised when I saw both Carlos *and* Bruno accompanying me out the door. Although perplexed, I didn't mind at all that two policemen instead of one were heading with me to the hostel.

The lady who initially denied my refund registered a look of shock when she saw me walking in the door with two policemen at my side. She didn't even wait for the officers or me to say anything to her. She just hightailed it to the back and called out to her supervisor. Together, they returned to the front, both of them appearing more than apprehensive about this turn of events. Apparently, they must have thought I was bluffing when I said I was going to get the police.

Carlos initiated the contact. In Spanish, he asked the supervisor what happened. In Spanish, she answered him. Their conversation was long and winding. Bit by bit, however, I could see that the tide was going my way.

Had it been an open and shut case on behalf of the hostel, I'm sure Carlos would have turned to me after he got the supervisor's version and said, "You're in the wrong. They're in the right. You don't deserve a refund." As it were, they were going back and forth which told me that the issue wasn't so cut and dry. Furthermore, I could tell from Bruno's facial expression that he didn't like what he was hearing. His eyes never shifted over to me to size me up; they always stayed focused on the supervisor. His face was becoming more contorted by the minute, and that told me that the supervisor's retelling in her own words wasn't doing her any favors.

Finally, Carlos brought the discussion to an end. He turned to me and stated with some resignation: "She said the rules on the website are wrong. After you pay, there is no refund."

Upon hearing that, my hopes deflated faster than you could say, "Nice try, bucko. Better luck next time." Disheartened, I gave it one last shot. "You mean they can put the rules on their website and then ignore them?" I asked Carlos.

Carlos gave me a sympathetic nod and added, "Sorry."

That was that, I concluded. I tried my best. I tried to get the refund I was due, and when I couldn't get the job done myself, I went and enlisted the help of the police. That too failed. There was nothing more I could do. As I prepared to walk away empty-handed, I shook my head and relinquished a rueful laugh. "Okay," I told Carlos, "thanks anyway." I started to go get my belongings from my room when Bruno suddenly surprised all of us.

With a stern countenance, he leaned into the supervisor and tore in to her like a starving pit bull going after a slab of raw steak. His unexpected attack and her hurried defense resulted in a flurry of back and forth exchanges entirely in Spanish. I didn't know what either one of them was saying, but that didn't hinder me from comprehending the gist of their sudden clash.

And if I were to translate what they said in English, I would verbalize the scuffle in the following way:

Snarling, Bruno demanded to know from the supervisor: "What do you mean you won't give him his money back?"

The woman without any scruples hurriedly answered, "It's like I just told the other officer. We don't give out refunds!"

"Was it true what this Chinese guy said?" Bruno countered as he gestured towards me. (I can safely assume he was referring to me as "Chinese" because I could have sworn I heard "Chino" – Spanish for "Chinese" – in there somewhere.) "Does your website say you would keep the first night's stay and refund the rest?"

The supervisor's response was noticeably weak. "Yes, but . . ."

"But nothing!" Bruno cut in, pounding his fist on the counter. (He actually pounded his fist on the counter.) "If that's your policy, then you give him back his money!"

At this point, I caught the look on the faces of the other hostel guests who happened to be in the lobby. Judging by their worrisome expression, I could tell that they were thinking the same thing I was. All of us were amassing a mutual concern: *Bruno was going overboard and was about to lose it!*

Don't get me wrong. I was glad he was fighting for my cause, but I was fearful he was going too far. It's one thing to argue over money. It's another thing to cause physical harm over money.

As the argument deepened, Bruno kept leaning in towards the supervisor, yelling at her, practically frothing at the mouth. It had gotten so bad that Carlos was stepping in between them and patting his colleague on the arm, saying something of a soothing nature to calm down his older colleague.

Whether the supervisor finally saw the error of her ways, or whether she was becoming fearful for her safety in the face of a looming onslaught by an angry policeman, she abruptly did an about face.

"Okay, okay! I will give him the refund!" she cried out.

Bruno eased in his attack but remained where he was, leaning forward, his eyes boring into the trembling culprit and his nose flaring at the offense she tried to inflict on the poor, innocent, unsuspecting tourist. (Hey, it's my version of the story and I can heap as much sympathy on myself as I want to.)

The next thing I knew, the woman was opening her cash register and yanking out a bunch of bills. Hastily, she counted out a sum that appeared to be the correct amount then slapped the bills down on the counter in front of me. "Take your refund!" she told me.

"Thanks," I said as I collected what was rightfully mine. With the money safely in my hands, I turned to Carlos and Bruno. "And thank you," I offered them, extremely grateful for their intervention.

Carlos nodded a "You're welcome" at me, but Bruno didn't say anything. He was still holding the supervisor in his angry stare, probably disappointed that she'd given in so easily and denying him the opportunity to unleash the full wrath of his fury upon her.

The younger policeman patted his partner on the arm again and gestured towards the door. With significant effort, not unlike that of separating a pit bull from his slab of steak, Bruno released the woman from his stare and allowed himself to be guided out the door.

An awkward moment ensued. Once the officers were gone, an icy silence spread throughout the hostel lobby. I could feel the two women behind the counter staring at me, their faces seething with disdain. I turned to them, not terribly surprised to see that the fear that was on their faces moments ago was now replaced with a renewed sense of anger.

I was tempted to say to them, "See? If you had refunded my money at the beginning like I asked, none of this would have happened." But I'm not one to gloat, at least not on the outside. I knew when to take my money and run, so I did. Without further adieu, I went to my room, got my bags, and vacated the premises.

The stay at the *pension* turned out to be quite nice. Having a room to myself provided a comfort I wouldn't have had at the hostel. And who do I have to thank for that? A certain Barcelona *Policia* who proved that being a policeman – a fence sitter who can intervene with a fair hand (although a bit emotionally in this case) – can be of much benefit to a tourist in need.

Gracias, Barcelona Bystanders

As much as I want to say I did not have a need for the *Policia* again for my stay in Barcelona, I can't. As it so happened, I did have cause to call upon them a second time. (I swear I didn't come to Spain to raise a ruckus.) When this second incident occurred, it made me glad I was able to dial down my fervor and engage in some beneficial, neutral thinking.

After having settled into my room at the *pension*, I paid a visit to the Pablo Picasso Museum. All in all, it was a mind-ruminating experience. I can't say I was able to comprehend and appreciate everything I saw. For instance, what was up with that "blue period" of Picasso's? And why did shading a piece of art in blue inherently give it a special significance? Would shading that same piece of art in green have also given it a special significance? Despite my reluctance to go along with the explanation of all the exhibits, I did enjoy the tour and was reflecting on what I observed when I plopped myself down on a bench in a park across the street from the museum. My mid-day hunger pangs had gotten the better of me, so right after I exited the museum, I went straight to one of the many food vendors nearby, bought myself a sandwich and a Coke, and added my company to a handful of people who were innocently lounging about the park, or at least I thought that's what all of them there were doing.

The sky was blue. The sun was shining. The birds were singing. The . . .

Okay, okay, I'll stop it with the depictions of a perfect day, but can you blame me? I'd just visited the museum of a world-renowned artist and was ensconced on a park bench with a sandwich in one hand, a Coke in the other, and I had nothing more to do than lazily lap up the scenery with my backpack lying next to me on the bench.

With everything that was going right, what could possibly go wrong?

If only I had asked myself that very question before setting myself up as a hapless victim – and an Asian victim at that (you'll see later why I point this out) – I wouldn't have had to learn a valuable lesson in travel the hard way.

As my mind was languidly drifting off to . . . who knows what . . . all of a sudden, I heard someone yelling, "Chino! Hey Chino!" (Yep, there's that word for "Chinese" again.) I jerked my head to the right and saw a guy in his early twenties of Middle-Eastern descent waving his hands up and down, while maintaining his yell of, "Chino! Hey, Chino!"

Then just as abruptly as he started yelling at me, he abruptly stopped. Then he turned around and took off running – away from me.

In a few blinks of an eye, several thoughts zipped through my mind. To the best of my memory, the order of their occurrence was:

1) Why was this guy calling me "Chinese?" Didn't he know I was Vietnamese?
2) Why the heck was he calling out to me and waving his arms up and down like that?
3) Why did he suddenly run *away* from me? He wouldn't have called out to me and run *away* from me . . . unless . . . oh (expletive)! . . . he was trying to distract me!

I jerked my head to the left and looked down at my backpack. It was gone!

I jumped up!

I looked to my left and right, all the while thinking: *No, don't tell me I've just been robbed!*

As much as I didn't want to admit it, that was exactly what happened. While one guy was distracting me, the other guy snuck up behind me and ran off with my backpack.

The feeling of being a victim was sickening.

I couldn't believe it. *I just got robbed!*

Then out of nowhere, I heard a woman's voice, shouting, "You! You!" I turned in the direction of the voice. A few people were having coffee on an outdoor terrace of a small café near the entrance to the park. One of them, a woman in her fifties, had jumped up and was motioning to me while pointing in the direction of the busy street that ran in front of the museum. It took me a second to read the urgent look on her face – one that was almost as frantic as mine. It was a look that that said: "The guy who snatched your backpack went that way!"

I bolted down the street, turned the corner, and came to a dead halt when I saw a sea of tourists in front of me. The thief was nowhere in sight. I stood and stared, hoping to spot something that would clue me in to the presence of my perpetrator. My frantic search was fruitless. I couldn't see the guilty guy anywhere.

The sinking feeling that crashed over me was akin to that of a certain gigantic ship hitting an even more gigantic iceberg. Without a doubt, I knew my backpack was gone for good.

Damning myself for not being more vigilant of my possessions while cursing the culprits who made me pay the price of idiotic negligence, I turned around and went back to the park. Having just witnessed a cancerous part of society, I was more than dejected. Fortunately for me, I was quickly reminded that a benevolent part of society also exists.

The woman who'd alerted me was waiting for me at the café. When she saw me coming back empty-handed, she and the man whom I assume was her husband rose from their seats and greeted me with sympathetic eyes. She motioned for me to have a seat at their table. In the following precious minutes, she would guide me through a series of actions what would assist me in recuperating the financial loss of my belongings and, possibly, the retention of my physical well-being as well.

Spanish, as I mentioned, is a language in which I am ignorant. That imposed a linguistic barrier for our ensuing dialogue. The barrier was challenging, but it wasn't insurmountable. Through a combination of the non-verbal facets like facial expressions and hand gestures, plus an overall absorption of the situation, I was able to glean the essence of our conversation. In light of that innate comprehension, I believe I can accurately recount our exchange in English as:

"He got away?" the woman asked me with empathy.

I nodded. "Yes."

"That's terrible! Terrible!" she declared emphatically.

Her husband agreed. "Yes! Terrible!"

I nodded again, all the while thinking, *Now what?* In that backpack were my camcorder, eyeglasses, and the manuscript for a personal memoir book I was editing – all gone in a single snatch. Luckily, my stash of money and passport were safely tucked away in my room back at the *pension*. None of the stolen items had left me in dire straits. Nevertheless . . . I still couldn't help thinking, *Now what?*

The woman whom I'll go ahead and refer to as "Maria," (and her husband as "Albert") must have read the look on my face, for they said the word *Policia* and waved to a waitress who'd come out onto the terrace. I looked on as Maria told the waitress what happened. I watched as the expression on the waitress' face metamorphosed from "What's the matter?" to "Oh, my God! They stole his backpack?"

At the end of Maria's report, the waitress (a rather attractive gal, I might add) nodded with a look of determination. Right before she hurried back into the café, she flashed me a look of empathy. As much as I would have liked the look to have said . . . "You poor thing. After this is over, I'll take you out on a special date and show you the town!" . . . I know in reality that the look actually said, "You poor thing. I'll call the cops right now and hopefully they can catch those crooks."

Minutes inched by while we waited for the authorities to arrive. Normally, I would have made some small talk with Maria and Albert, but all I could do was relive those shocking seconds in which my backpack was virtually yanked out from right under my nose. Over and over, I simultaneously asked myself how I could have let such a thing happen, and how could such a thing have happened to me? I'm not sure how long I was stuck in that self-loathing, self-pitying state of mind when an unexpected development snapped me out of it.

Suddenly, I heard Maria gasping, "He's back!"

Puzzled, I looked up from the spot on the ground I'd been staring at. I saw Maria looking across the park with an expression of shock, anger, and outright disgust. I followed her gaze, and when I saw what she saw, I also gained an expression of shock, anger, and outright disgust.

Believe it or not, standing on the far side of the park was none other than the guy who had waved at me and yelled "Chino!" to distract me. He was just standing there, looking nonchalant, acting as though he'd done nothing wrong.

No, wait, let me rephrase that.

He was just standing there, looking nonchalant, acting as though he knew he'd done something wrong and not giving a damn because he knew there wasn't anything I could do about it.

The nerve of his audacity raised my hackles. I couldn't believe the son of a bitch! He was brazenly broadcasting that he stole my backpack from me and now he was daring me to go after him. If it was a fight he was looking for, then it was a fight he was gonna get!

I sprang up from my chair and took a step in his direction – only to have Maria put her hand on my arm and tell me to stop right there. Befuddled, I looked at her with an expression that said: *What are you doing?*

Maria shook her head vigorously. With a hand firmly gripped around the handle of a pretend knife, she made several stabbing motions at my stomach. Her message to me was undeniably clear: *You go over there, and those guys will stab you to death!*

A quick survey of the dilapidated apartment buildings behind my perpetrator told me I would be wise to heed Maria's warning. The setting looked bleak, troubled. They spoke of a squalor that only the impoverished can attest to. It was a squalor I knew well, for at one point in my family's history, it was in such a fetid place that we had to call home.

Poverty can have different effects on people. It can make them work twice as hard to get themselves out of the financial hardship they're in – or it can make them steal, plunder, and commit who knows what to put ill-gotten goods into their pocket. It didn't take a degreed sociologist to register which path my perpetrator had taken.

Call me a coward, but I quickly accepted Maria's advice. I sat my butt right back down in that chair and didn't move a muscle. The scenario that hurtled through my mind was too realistic, too threatening, to allow me to do otherwise. As I was walking to the Picasso Museum earlier that day, I could tell that the area wasn't the best of neighborhoods. One glimpse at the run-down apartment buildings like the ones on the far side of that park told me that I would be wise to watch my back.

Once I was re-seated and using more of my cranial resources, I stared at the menacing buildings on the opposite side of the park and pictured the predicament that would have confronted me if I'd been foolish enough to disregard Maria's warning, a predicament that would have surely ended badly for me. If I'd run over there to catch the guy who was flaunting his guilt, he probably would have bolted in the pretense of eluding me. Eventually, he would have led me into a labyrinth of maze-like alleyways. Once I was good and lost in my futile pursuit, he would have stopped and turned around to reveal a sinister smile. Out of the shadows, his accomplices would have appeared, one of them unveiling a knife that he would wield deftly, wickedly, to make me regret I was senseless enough to chase after my perpetrator. Slowly but assuredly, my assailants would have closed in on me like a noose around a hapless neck. Scornfully, they would have laughed at me while saying, "If you think it was bad that we took your backpack, just wait until we take your life!"

I may not have the highest I.Q. around, but I know when I would be putting myself in grave jeopardy. The bad guys had already shown me how easily they could run away with my property. I wasn't about to let them show me how easily they could also run away with my life. Furthermore, and although this won't bolster my macho image in any way, I'll be the first to admit I'm much more of a writer than a fighter. A fighter's definition of a good day's work is to knock somebody out with a mean, right hook. For a writer like me, the definition of a good day's work is to come up with a sentence that has really good subject-verb agreement.

With some effort, I tore my eyes away from the offender across the park, still taunting me with his blatant presence.

Minutes later, two policemen arrived. As soon as they showed up, I checked to see if the guy who necessitated their arrival was still loitering around so I could point him out to the cops. Of course, he wasn't.

At that point, there wasn't anything more to do except give the policemen my account of what happened and hope for the best. As it turned out, the best did meet my hopes.

Like I mentioned, I'd never stayed in a hostel before. Not knowing what to expect, I bought travelers insurance in case something went wrong. As it turned out, something did go wrong, and that made my insurance purchase a very fortunate one.

As soon as I returned to my home in Southern California, I filed a claim for my losses. Afterwards, I told my friend who's in the insurance business about the theft and informed him of the claim I filed. To my surprise, he told me there's a good chance the insurance company will refuse to pay. When I asked him why, he said the business is rife with fraud. He stated that anybody could purchase some insurance, have something "happen" to them during the trip, then file a claim to retrieve the money they never lost. I could see his point and prepared myself for a battle with the insurance company. To my further surprise, the battle never materialized. The insurance company sent me a check to cover my losses without a peep of protest. Upon reflection, I'm fairly certain I know why they didn't object, and the reason has to do with the bystanders at that café in Barcelona.

When the policemen arrived to get a report, I discovered that their English was about as good as my Spanish — nonexistent. It was Maria and Albert who stepped in and spoke to them on my behalf. It was those two good Samaritans who told the policemen what happened. It was Maria and Albert who gave them an eyewitness account of how one thief distracted me while the other ran off with my backpack. Without my benefactors' intervention, the policemen might have ended up with a shoddy report, or no report at all, given how I was incapable of communicating with them.

As it was, Maria and Albert were on hand to give them a detailed account of the theft in all of its inglorious details which allowed the policemen to get a comprehensive account of the crime and fully document the circumstances of the theft. That in turn led to the detailed report that verified the authenticity of my claim to the insurance company, and it was that proof on file that told the insurance company that my loss was genuine and that they had to fulfill their fiduciary duty and reimburse me for my losses.

Lastly, there was that bit I mentioned earlier about being an Asian victim in Barcelona. Before I started my trip, I read in one of the guidebooks that Barcelona has one of the highest crime rates against tourists in Europe, and for some particular reason, the highest demographics of the victims are Asians. While it crossed my mind that I too could fall prey to the elements of crime and contribute to that statistic, I quickly brushed aside the idea as implausible. I was too well-traveled, I told my pompous self. I was too well-learned in the ways of the world, I convinced my idiotic self. I was too wary to be snookered, I said to my delusional self. And look what happened. I ended up as yet another hapless victim, another statistic to bolster the fact that most of the tourists who fall prey to the criminal element in Barcelona are indeed Asians.

Ever since that unfortunate ordeal, I've learned a thing or two about thwarting the claws of the criminally-minded, and it's a lesson I hope you'll allow me to pass on to you. When you're out and about, always keep your belongings in front of you where they'll be in your line of sight. Better yet, keep your belongings in front of you *and* keep your arm around a bag strap or something like that so you are physically connected to your property. That way, you can see *and* feel the theft the instant it happens. Not only will this immediately alert you to the crime, it may prevent the crime itself. The bad guys are constantly scoping the crowd to determine who is the most vulnerable. If they see that you've got an arm around your belongings and that your property is in your line of sight, they'll see that you're not an easy mark and will be less likely to rob you.

Most of all, if something bad happens to you and your emotions are running rampant, recognize that you're prone to doing something that may fracture the situation further instead of fixing it, like running after a thief who's blatantly flaunting his presence on the other side of the park. That's when you'll want to listen to the advice of the wiser people around you, like a woman who's telling you to sit your butt down so you won't get stabbed to death. That way, you can brush off the incident as a lesson well-learned. That way, you'll maintain your well-being so you can continue to travel the world and feast your eyes on its many wonders. That way, you'll gain the benefit of clear, neutral thinking.

Captain Cuckoo

Our red-eye flight from Las Vegas to Washington, DC pushed back from the gate a few minutes before midnight. We flight attendants showed the safety demonstration then walked through the cabin to do our safety checks as usual. Not surprisingly, I saw that virtually all the passengers had settled into their seats and closed their eyes, apparently more than ready to take advantage of the flight that blended in with their bedtime. As the passengers prepared to snooze their way to the East Coast, we turned off the lights so the dark interior would match the dark exterior. (In case you're curious, we match the interior lighting with the exterior lighting so that in case of an emergency evacuation, you won't need a few extra seconds to adjust your eyes to a different level of lighting as you rush out the door.) Then all four of us flight attendants secured ourselves into our jumpseats, the retractable seats by the doors where we sit for take-off and landing. On this particular flight, my assigned jumpseat was at the front of the plane, so I took a seat next to the other flight attendant who was assigned to that door.

A sharp turn told me we had come out of the alleyway and were proceeding to the runway. I expected us to be airborne within minutes.

Normally, I would chit-chat with the flight attendant next to me. Tonight, however, I didn't have much to say to my colleague who happened to also be the Lead Attendant for the flight. He was a middle-aged man who'd been at his job (unhappily, it appeared) for over a decade and would have to keep at it for at least another decade before he could claw at the boundary of early retirement. Some people wear their emotions on their sleeves. This guy wore his grumpiness on his chest. One deep frown from him, and the passengers would know to keep their distance.

The silence at our jumpseats seeped into the exhaustive silence that blanketed the cabin. That was fine with me. No matter what the source of silence was, a quiet cabin was nevertheless a quiet cabin, and when it came to a travel mode where crammed-in people can get cantankerous, a quiet cabin is never a bad thing.

As the plane picked up some noticeable speed, it occurred to me that we had been taxiing for an unusually long period of time. It crossed my mind that we should have reached the runway by now and that the captain should have come over the P.A. to make his usual "Flight attendants, prepare for take-off" announcement. He hadn't, so I just chalked it up to the possibility that we were using the farthest runway from the terminal. As it turned out, we were – although when I eventually did find out that was the case, I wished the captain had kept the development to himself, or at least have shared it with only the crew.

I don't recall the name of our captain, nor do I care to, because in my mind, he will always be "Captain Cuckoo."

I'm sure Captain Cuckoo had traveled as a passenger on a few red-eye flights himself. I'm sure he had sat in the quiet cabin with the lights turned down and seen that practically everyone onboard was entering their sleep mode. I'm sure that if he'd employed some common sense, he wouldn't have done anything to disturb them – including delivering a piece of abrupt, disturbing news. I guess he left his common sense back at the gate because as we continued to make our way towards the runway, he suddenly came on the PA and announced: "This is your captain speaking. Believe it or not, we were almost to our designated runway when Air Traffic Control told us we had to change to another runway. They said there was a man shooting off a machine gun at the end of our original runway. Now we have to turn around and go to a farther runway."

I found the news about a man firing a machine gun to be, of course, disturbing. Yet perhaps just as disturbing was how the captain indiscriminately announced such an unexpected turn of events to the passengers. It wasn't as if the travelers onboard could have done anything about the matter, and since they couldn't do anything about it, why blare the disconcerting incident recklessly throughout the entire plane? The captain should have exercised a need-to-know discretion, especially when it involved a piece of information that was so potentially alarming.

To be perfectly candid about it, right after Captain Cuckoo made his announcement, I thought to myself: *What was he thinking? Not only did he wake up the passengers with a very loud and prolonged announcement, but he also delivered some upsetting news – news that he should have kept to himself or shared discreetly with only the crew.*

As I feared, within seconds of that announcement, a call button lit up in the cabin. I peered into the darkness and saw that someone seated near the overwing exits was asking for assistance. Since the Lead Attendant is supposed to oversee everything in the cabin, I assumed my colleague next to me would get up and see what the call button was about. To my dismay, he just sat there. In the small chance that he truly didn't see the lit up call button, I played dumb and asked him, "Is that a call button on in the middle of the cabin?"

His reply was terse: "Yeah."

A palpable moment hobbled by as I expected him to either say more or do more. When he didn't, I said unabashedly, "Are you going to answer it?"

"No," he said quickly while folding his arms across his chest as if to emphasize his refusal.

I shook my head in disbelief. This guy who was getting extra pay to be the Lead was shirking his responsibilities and not giving a damn. To make matters worse, he was seated next to the aisle whereas I was seated between him and the door, practically wedged into a crevice. He had much easier access to the cabin than I had and could easily take a few steps down the aisle to take care of the issue. Since he didn't see fit to address the matter, I took it upon myself to get it done.

Mimicking a contortionist, I unfastened the horizontal seatbelt across my lap and loosened the two harnesses strapped

55

vertically over my shoulders. Being careful not to bump my head on the inward-curving door to my right, I got up, stepped over the extended legs of my lazy coworker, and went down the aisle, being careful to balance myself while the plane continued to roll speedily towards the runway.

The passenger who pushed the call button was a young man who looked like he was a year shy of his twentieth birthday. "Can I help you?" I asked him while noticing that his eyes were enlarged with concern and his face was filled with fret.

He leaned forward and exclaimed in a shaking voice, "I want to get off the plane!"

I had no doubt that the shrapnel from Captain Cuckoo's announcement was why this young man wanted to evacuate the aircraft. Despite that forgone conclusion, I went ahead and asked him what the issue was to be sure. "Why? What's the matter?" I said.

"The captain just said somebody's shooting a machine gun! I don't want to get shot! I want to get off the plane!"

I nodded to show I understood his concern. "I don't think there's any real danger," I relayed with a calm voice that I hoped would help calm him down. "If you'd like, I can double-check with the captain."

"Okay. Can you do that?"

"Sure."

I knew that many passengers who make up the flying public – especially the young and easily impressionable ones like the petrified passenger before me – perceive the captain to be the know-all and end-all authority figure on the airplane. I knew that if I visibly consulted with the captain and reported his decision back to the young man, my frightened passenger would be much more acceptable of the situation and be put much more at ease. "Be right back," I told him as I walked to the front of the plane, picked up the phone, and called the captain – all while noticeably standing in the middle of the aisle so that the fearful young man could see I was actively addressing the matter.

"Yes?" Captain Cuckoo said in gruff voice when he answered my call.

I was tempted to ask him, "*What the hell were you thinking when you made that stupid announcement!*" Knowing full well I couldn't do that, I instead stated, "A passenger wants to get off the plane because he's scared about the machine gun. What should I tell –"

"Tell them that's not going to happen," Captain Cuckoo spat out as he cut me off. "We didn't come all the way out here just to go back to the gate!"

The curtness in his tone was pretty much what I expected to hear. Admittedly, before I picked up the phone to call him, I did have high hopes of asking him to make another announcement to smooth out the first one, but even if he'd been open to that request, I wasn't sure if I would have gone through with it. I wasn't sure if I could trust him *not* to make another announcement that was also entirely inappropriate. I wasn't sure if I could trust him *not* to say something reckless like: "Ladies and gentlemen, as I said earlier, there was a guy shooting off a machine gun. Now there's another crazy person out there throwing grenades. For all we know, there could be yet another maniac firing off a bazooka at all the aircrafts within a hundred yards. If I were you, I would look for a good place to duck and cover!"

As it was, the only option I had was to tell the fearful passenger he couldn't get off the plane. I told Captain Cuckoo, "Got it," and hung up, only too glad to curtail my contact with him. Succinctly, I went back to the young man who was anxiously waiting to hear from me. When I reached his seat, he was still leaning forward with his eyes widened and his face full of concern. "I just talked to the captain," I informed the young man. "It's not a big deal. We'll be out of here in no time."

His trepidation visibly downshifted to a normal state. "Okay. Thanks. Sorry to bother you."

"It's not a big deal. We're gonna take off any second now."

"Great. Okay."

Relieved that he was relieved, I returned to my seat. On my way there, I thankfully heard the words from the captain that made my words to the young man true: "Flights attendants, prepare for take-off."

I climbed over the extended legs of the Lead Attendant, buckled myself into my jumpseat, and got ready to fly away from the man brandishing a machine gun at the runway – a fact that should have never been made to the public.

For the rest of the flight, aside from my lazy colleague doing the very least that he could, everything went well. There were no more unusual incidents, nothing to provoke the captain to making an asinine announcement.

When I think back to this unusual occurrence, I can't help but wish that the captain had chosen the path of non-action. If he had, he would have spared a certain passenger a very big scare. If he had, he would have allowed that young man to gain the benefits of neutral thinking.

"I'm Ready To Go!"

I just thought of another instance where non-action can be beneficial, and I'll have to ask for your indulgence while I tack on this particular non-occurrence. After the infamous date of 9/11, a number of commercial airplanes were staffed with Federal Air Marshals, commonly known within the airline industry as "FAMs," to guard against another disastrous hijacking. These days, the vast majority of the flights with FAMs onboard are uneventful, so much so that I would wager that 99.99% of them start and end with a ho-hum yawn. One flight that came about a few years after 9/11, unfortunately, was the exception, as it involved a bizarre turn of events that had nothing to do with terrorism.

The details of this sad event are sketchy and conflicting. What is certain is that after the plane had landed and was in the vicinity of the gate, a man who would later be described as "sick" rushed towards the cockpit. For reasons that aren't clear, the undercover FAMs onboard mistook his actions as malevolent, drew their weapons, and shot him to death. From the subsequent reports, I can't help but come to the conclusion that the FAMs' zeal got the better of them, causing them to overreact and creating a fatality.

Several years after this incident, something similar happened on a flight I worked. The result, thankfully, was much less severe.

I was the Lead Attendant on the flight. That placed me at the front of the plane, right next to the cockpit door.

After the plane had landed, I made the usual announcement to the passengers, part of which was reminding everyone to stay seated while the plane progressed to the gate. After I finished the announcement, I turned towards the window, idly looking out while passing the time.

All of a sudden, I heard, "I'm ready to go!"

I whipped my head around. To my amazement, there was a passenger standing in the aisle, holding his two carry-on bags in his hands, all set to get off the plane. I regarded the young man who was about twenty-five years old with blonde hair, dressed in a T-shirt and shorts – and wearing an odd, crooked grin.

"Um, uh," I responded slowly while thinking of the best way to deal with this unusual surprise. As I assessed the situation, the focus of my attention kept coming back to his off-kilter smile. I couldn't help it. His countenance was so crooked, so unnerving, that it made me wonder if he was "sick" somehow.

While this passenger continued to grin at me like a jack-o-lantern carved cantankerously, I stated the obvious to him: "We're still taxiing, and we're taxiing pretty fast too. You should return to your seat."

I braced myself for an objection. I readied myself for an outburst. I prepared myself to hear him yell, "But I wanna get off the plane NOW!"

Instead, he simply said, "Okay," then pivoted in a spiffy way, and immediately went back to his seat – all the while still exhibiting his crooked grin.

I leaned into the aisle to watch him march to the back of coach. In addition to making sure he would return to his seat, I also wanted to sure he wouldn't do anything abnormal like taking a quick detour to the overwing exit and throwing open the emergency window to jump out of the plane headfirst. Of course, throughout this little episode, I was wondering: *What the heck is this guy thinking?*

As you might have guessed, I wasn't the only person having this thought.

While I was making sure the eager-to-exit passenger wasn't making any dangerous detours, I noticed that every single passenger on the plane was doing the exact, same thing I was doing – staring at this oddball character with a mixture of bewilderment and wariness. Everyone was craning their necks looking at him, befuddled as to why it even entered his head to try and get off the plane while it was still speeding across the tarmac.

Watching them watching him, I'm fairly certain they concluded that their fellow passenger was someone who required special handling. As a matter of fact, they might have formulated the same thought I had. They might have speculated that if this guy were to check into a hotel later that day and hung up a "Do Not Disturb" sign outside his door, the hotel staff would quietly approach his room and replace his sign with another one that read: "DO NOT DISTURB THE DISTURBED."

Once I was assured my roaming passenger was seated again, it dawned on me that among all the passengers looking bewildered and wary were the FAMs who happened to be onboard. My initial reaction was to be thankful that they were there in case the vexing occurrence became confrontational. My other, almost simultaneous reaction, was to be thankful that the FAMs did exactly what they should have done: *Nothing.*

My mind jogged back to the lethal incident in the news, the one about the passenger who was shot dead by the over eager FAMs, and I was glad the FAMs on my flight weren't anything like the FAMs on that flight. Instead of jumping in and reacting with extreme measure, the FAMs on my flight stayed seated to see how the passenger would respond to my request to return to his seat. They waited to see if their involvement would be necessary. When they saw it wasn't, they chose the path of non-action as their best course of action.

What happened afterwards, you may be asking?

Minutes later, the plane came to a complete stop and parked at the gate. All the passengers disembarked as usual, including the overzealous young man still sporting his oddly etched grin. As a result, the flight ended like 99.99% of the other flights . . . with a ho-hum yawn.

Neutrally Naturally

In case you're under the impression that being neutral is something that applies only to people, take a look at the ways of nature. You'll see that there being neutral is also something that applies to nature.

~

When cats have babies, they often move their kittens to a hidden place to keep them out of harm's way. Cats, of course, can't walk upright like people do, and they certainly don't have hands. That makes them unable to carry their babies like we human beings can. So how does a mother cat move her kittens? As you may well know, she bites them on the back of the neck, but the bite isn't a full bite. It's a part-way bite, a neutral sort of bite. It's a partial bite done with just enough force to exert sufficient pressure on the kitten's neck to allow for grasping but not enough to inflict the least bit of harm. It's a safe bet that the mother cat didn't learn how to do this by attending Mommy Cat School. It's a safe bet that she knows how to do this because nature has embedded in her the instinct to act neutrally naturally.

~

It's not only the feline females who gently care for their young with their jaws. Alligators do it too. After about nine weeks of incubation, the baby alligators will start to emerge from their eggs. They'll emit a grunting noise that lets their mother know they're ready for their introduction to planet Earth. The mommy gator will take an egg in her mouth, lightly roll it around with her tongue, and gently crack open the egg to help the baby emerge from the shell more easily.

For the next several months, possibly up to a year, all the baby alligators will remain at their mother's side. At the slightest sign of danger, the mother alligator will open her jaws part way and keep it open in a neutral manner to allow her babies to swim into her mouth and stay there until the danger has passed. Due to the partially opened jaws that are neither fully clamped nor completely open, the dagger-like teeth that are capable of ferociously tearing a large prey apart become a haven for the tiny newborns.

~

Although being neutral as human beings can be a conscious act (as in we deliberately initiate an undertaking), it can also be a subconscious act (as in it happens on its own). Take, for example, our natural body temperature. At 98.6°, our body is at just the right temperature, and that allows us to walk around smiling like a bunch of clams that just avoided the chowder pot. We're so comfortable at those digits that we could be the proverbial porridge that Goldilocks found in the house of Papa Bear, Mama Bear, and Baby Bear – not too hot, not too cold, just right. If that temperature starts dropping, however, then we start shivering to warm up our bodies to an agreeable 98.6°. If that temperature starts rising, then we start sweating to cool down to a sensible 98.6°. Whatever the case may be, our bodies will react subconsciously to make sure we're at the right setting, neutrally naturally.

~

I hate to "mouth" off to you, but while writing this book, I came across a news story that I had to pass on to you. It involved the jaws of a particular animal and how, once again, being neutral was of a great benefit. In Savannah, Georgia there was a small Chihuahua dog named Chachi and a Pit Bull dog named Joani. Both of them were living on the streets. Chachi suffered a bad eye infection. The injury got so bad that the eye ruptured. Injured, weakened, and half-blind, Chachi had a lot trouble getting around on his own, so his soul mate Joani stepped in and offered him a lift – with her jaws.

Like a mother cat that would carry her kittens in her mouth and like an adult alligator that would partly close its mouth over her babies to provide protection, Joani the Pit Bull would employ a neutral frame of mind and gingerly close her mouth over the back of Chachi's neck to lift him up and move him from place to place. Like her animal cousins, Joani exerted only enough force in her bite to be helpful, not harmful. In doing so, she also demonstrated the benefit of being neutrally naturally.

~

In the animal kingdom, the need to breed can be a powerful drive. The reindeer in Norway are no exception. During the mating season, also known as a "rut," the bulls are so driven by the urge to mate that they can engage in severe battles with each other and inflict severe injuries upon one another. The driving force behind this aggression is the testosterone rampaging through their bodies, and the source of this testosterone are the animals' testicles.

To prevent rampant fighting during a rut, the reindeer keepers castrate their reindeer, but they do it in a unique way. They don't remove both testicles. They "half-castrate" the animals by removing only one testicle. By taking away half of the raw force of the testosterone, the keepers get a more docile reindeer that doesn't fight nearly as much. Moreover, by leaving the reindeer with one testicle, the keepers provide for a more positive effect of the testosterone, namely the promotion of muscle growth. The result is that the half-castrated reindeer can become bigger than their peers that weren't castrated at all because they don't exhaust their bodily energy – precious energy that can build up body mass – by jousting and fighting to satisfy their mating desires. This build-up in bulk can come in handy when the snowfall gets heavy. At these times, the half-castrated, bigger reindeer can use their larger mass to better dig out the grass from beneath the ice and snow. Furthermore, their more compliant demeanor makes them more likely to share their food with the young calves in the herd, thus helping the herd as a whole.

Plainly, there's something to be said for doing something halfway, for reaching a neutral middle ground, and getting the best overall results.

And now for the kicker – or should I say "biter." Yes, you read that right. There is biting involved, and unless you want to read something really cringe-worthy, you might want to skip the next few sentences, especially if you're a guy. In certain parts of Norway, the veterinarians don't castrate the reindeer by using any kind of surgical instruments. Nope, they keep it really simple. Once the reindeer is properly restrained, the veterinarian aims his teeth at the reindeer's nether region, grab a testicle between his teeth, and – gulp – bites down hard on the testicle!

Neutrally, Man-Made

Have you given any thought to how our society sometimes go out of our way to manufacture something that's neutral? There are a lot of everyday products all around us that are made to have a half-way effectiveness.

Have you ever torn a piece of paper in half? It's hard to make an exact tear along a specific line, isn't it? You might have folded the paper and pressed down on it to emphasize the crease, but even so, it's hard to make a precise tear unless you utilize a tool like a pair of scissors.

So if you don't have a pair of scissors handy, what's a good way to tear a piece of paper exactly in half?

By "pre-tearing" it, of course.

In other words, by using perforated paper.

Quite a few workplaces like mine use the scroll-type of printer paper. Before every flight, we flight attendants print a briefing sheet that has the pertinent information on it. Once the printing is done, we tear off the sheet and take it on the plane with us. If the sheet is a solid piece of paper, we would have to fold it and tear it and risk having a messy, jagged tear. A good way to avoid that is to use perforated paper.

I'm sure you know that perforated paper is paper with alternating holes along a specific line. If you think about it, those alternating little holes essentially make the paper halfway torn. The paper manufacturer, of course, did this on purpose. By intentionally compromising the integrity of the paper, by neutralizing its composition, the manufacturer provides a way for people like us flight attendants to conveniently tear off the briefing sheet along a specific line and quickly be on our merry way.

~

Along with neatly tearing apart a piece of paper, there's also the matter of sticking up a piece of paper. There are times when we want to strongly adhere a piece of paper to a surface, like a "For Sale" sign to a concrete wall. For these occasions, it would make sense to use a strong material like duct tape. There are also times when we don't want something so strong. There are times when we want a milder adhesion, like attaching a small piece of paper to a refrigerator door. For these instances, it wouldn't make sense to employ a material of industrial strength such as duct tape. No, it would be more practical to use something much milder, something like a Post-It note.

Surely, you've used these little notes yourself, so you know that they're great for short term uses and that they don't leave a sticky mess behind. Knowing that, you're aware that they're a great midpoint between totally non-sticking and completely strong-sticking. Recognizing that, you're apt to agree that a Post-It note exemplifies a man-made object that's effective by being neutral.

~

Paper isn't the only manufactured object bearing neutral integrity. It's not the only man-made object portraying the benefit of a perforation. There's also the bottle cap. Who hasn't turned the cap of a newly-purchased soda bottle and heard the tiny snapping sound as the top of the cap separated from the bottom? That snapping sound, as I'm sure you know, comes as a result of the perforation between the two parts of the cap. Since you don't live under a rock, I'm also sure you know that the perforation is a safeguard against the dangers of malicious tampering.

If an unsold bottle of soda can be opened without detection, it can be injected with a harmful substance then sold to an unsuspecting consumer. Subsequently, the marketplace needs a way to alert the consumer that a bottle has been opened. That's where a perforated bottle cap comes in very handy. If someone opens a bottle and doesn't hear the comforting sound of "snap-snap," she will know the bottle has been opened already. She will know that the bottle has been tampered with and to throw it away.

~

And then there's one of my favorite man-made objects: The airplane.

Aside from the take-off that requires the plane to be angled upwards and the landing that requires the plane to be angled downward, the best position for a passenger plane to be in is a level, neutral position. When we're in an airplane that's zooming along at 400 miles per hour at the height of 30,000 feet, we don't want the plane to be leaning to the far left or the far right, nor do we want the plane to pitch severely forward or backwards.

Huh-uh. We want the airplane to stay on an even keel so we can eat, drink, and sleep in comfort as if we were on flat, solid ground – and the best way to do that is through the utilitarian tools of the plane such as the horizontal stabilizer, the vertical stabilizer, the rudder, and of course, the wings. It is through the application of these instruments that we can enjoy our aerial ride in a level, neutral position.

~

There's something else that's man-made to consider, although this one is a procedure rather than an object. If you've ever bought a house, you know that it involves a lot of money. In a metropolitan area, the average price tag can run upwards of hundreds of thousands of dollars. As expected, the buyer and the seller are at opposite sides of the purchase process. Therefore, someone must act as a go-between in order to carry out the transaction in an unbiased manner. Someone must ensure that the huge amount of money goes where it's supposed to go. That third party is the Escrow Service. Without it, the buyer and seller who can be complete strangers wouldn't get anything done because they can't trust one another to act properly and legally. Without it, a lot of fraud would take place, and a lot of people would lose a lot of money due to rampant dishonesty.

With the Escrow Service fitted into place, people can rest assured that they can buy and sell a house worry-free because there is a neutral party that makes sure everything is done properly and legally.

~

Since we're in the area of procedures and man-made creations, I'd like to pass on a small discovery of mine. (Hey, you don't have to be manly to pass on a man-made creation, you know!) As someone who routinely stays in hotels as part of his job, I quickly ran into a problem during my first winter on my job. Many hotels don't have a quiet, central air heating system. Quite a few of them have those wall-mounted heaters that go off and on during the night. Unfortunately, when they come on, the motor is so loud that it's like a car revving up its engine. The result is that I can be fast asleep only to have the heater abruptly crank up its engine and jolt me awake.

One option I had was to turn off the heater altogether. I tried this but found out it didn't work too well. With the heater completely off, the room can get so cold that it wakes me up in the middle of the night, making me shiver and lose out on a good night's sleep. The other option was to stuff earplugs completely into my ears to totally shut out the sound. This alternative had a major drawback in that it worked *too* well. In addition to shutting out the sound of the belligerent heater, it also shut out the sound of my alarm clock. This, of course, was unacceptable because I couldn't risk waking up late for work.

What's a flight attendant to do?

I tried a halfway option, and it worked out just right. I put the earplugs halfway into my ears so that it blocked out only half the sound. This neutral method of mine sufficiently drowned out the boisterous noise from the heater and reduced it to an imperceptible, idling hum. More importantly, it allowed me to hear the alarm clock and wake up to go to work.

~

Every business must mind its expenses and try to keep its actions cost-neutral. The airline business has an added concern in that it must find a way to keep a certain aspect "space-neutral."

Since the planes are flying fuller these days, often filling up to make the passengers feel like sardines in a can, personal space has become more of a commodity than it has ever been. The most precious of this space is the area right in front of a seated passenger – and when that passenger has the seatback in front of him shoot back into his face, he can feel violated – justifiably or not. When tempers are already on edge from the sardine effect, this invasion of personal space can push a person over the edge.

I, like virtually every working flight attendant today, has had to settle disputes concerning this issue. (More and more, I feel that the true duty of my job is to settle conflicts, and that instead of coming to work in my flight attendant uniform, I should come to work wearing a referee uniform.) The problem isn't going away. On the contrary, it's here to stay because the new business model of the airlines is here to stay. As recently as the year 2000, airlines were increasing capacity (adding jumbo jets to their fleet) to accommodate the passengers. While this allowed more empty seats for the passengers to spread out once they're onboard, the added costs (aircrafts, staffing, catering, maintenance, etc.) was so prohibitive that it drove a number of the airlines into bankruptcy. Having learned their lesson, the carriers have reduced the number of aircrafts they use and are filling them with as many passengers as possible.

One time, on a red-eye flight I working, it was about 3 a.m. and we had been airborne for several hours. The entire plane was dark, and everyone was sleeping. I was in the back galley when I suddenly heard shouting coming from the middle of the coach cabin. I rushed out there to see what the matter was and came upon a woman and a man yelling at each other.

It turned out that the woman wanted to recline her seat, but the tall man behind her wouldn't let her because it cramped up his legs. Neither would budge in their position and that's when the shouting started. Once I'd gotten the full scoop of the situation, I had to deliver the bad news to the tall man. As much as I sympathized with him, I said, I can't force the woman to bring her seatback forward. As unfair as it may be, she has the right to recline her seat. Thankfully, the man understood where I was coming from and relented in his insistence, partly because he saw a viability in my suggestion that he could move his knees to the sides of the seat so they won't bear the full brunt of the reclined seatback. Eventually, both of them calmed down, and the flight continued uneventful.

The same cannot be said of the stories I've been hearing in the news. More and more, I've been reading about passengers getting into verbal arguments and physical altercations over reclined seats. The way things are going, I'm afraid a conflict will get chaotic enough to get someone seriously hurt, or even killed.

Perhaps it's time to reverse this trend by reversing the seating mechanism, thereby making the reclined seat "space-neutral."

As it is now, when a passenger reclines her seat, the top of her seatback moves backward – invading the personal space of the passenger behind her. We can avoid the potential conflict by applying a converse approach. Instead of having the top of the seatback move back, the bottom of the seatback – as well as the seat cushion part itself – should move forward. This would provide for the angled, reclined seat that the passenger wants without having any part of her seatback invading the space of the person behind her.

Admittedly, this would lessen the leg space of the person reclining her seat, but all things considered, it's a fair trade-off. Everyone onboard should have a set amount of personal space to work with. They can do with that space as they please. If they want to have a reclined seat in lieu of less leg room, that's their prerogative. As long as they don't encroach upon anyone else's space and cause any heated fisticuffs, everyone is a happy camper.

A Few More

At the risk of giving you whiplash, I have to yank you back to the topic of being neutral in the sense of doing nothing, particularly when doing something can be harmful.

A few years before starting this book, the airline that I work for merged with another airline. Afterwards, the newly-merged company began working on a new contract for my work group. It was common knowledge from that point on that management would most likely offer a buyout for the people with a lot of seniority. Subsequently, a lot of flight attendants who were in their sixties and seventies (and even eighties!) and eligible for retirement knew to wait and see what the buyout offered. They knew to remain neutral and do nothing for the time being.

All of them, that is, except one.

A woman who had been at her job for 45 years didn't like the way the new company was doing things. She didn't like the new management. She didn't like the new rules. She didn't like many of her new co-workers.

She wanted out.

She wasn't alone. Many of her senior peers also wanted out. But they also wanted to wait and see what the potential buyout would offer. So they bided their time, and they advised her to do the same. They also told her there were measures she could take to lessen her exposure to the new company, like reducing her work hours or taking a leave of absence, all the while keeping her name on the payroll.

She should have listened.

She didn't.

She quit.

This flight attendant with 45 years of seniority retired without any regard to the highly-speculated offer just around the corner.

Weeks after she retired, management unveiled the buyout everyone was expecting – and it was one, sweet deal!

The new company offered those who had at least 25 years of seniority $100,000 to retire.

That's right.

$100,000 just to stop working.

Consequently, the woman who exceeded the buyout seniority criteria by two decades lost out on a free $100,000 paycheck.

I'll bet anything that when she heard the news, she wanted to kick herself for not being neutral, for not doing nothing, so she could easily gain the benefit of $100,000.

~

Not too long ago, when I was perusing the internet, I happened to come across an article about the battle of Normandy on D-Day in World War II. As the moonlight traipsed down onto the beach that was the battlefield, the Higgins boats that carried the men and machinery of the Allied Forces approached the point of contact. The specially designed bows of these landing crafts dropped down to serve as a bridge between sea and shore. Methodically, the tanks on some of the boats rumbled off the boats, across the bridge, and onto the beach to meet the Nazi enemy. Sadly, some of the tanks rolled off the boats too soon and sank into waters that were too deep, consequently drowning the men inside.

The chaos of the battle must have been enormous, and I won't insult the memory of the soldiers who perished that day by second-guessing their premature departure from the boats. I only wish they'd been – somehow, some way – more of a fence sitter. I only wish they'd done nothing for a short while longer so their boats could have reached shallow shores and allowed the tanks to gain solid ground to provide them with a fighting chance.

~

74

Sometimes the person we're battling can be ourselves.

There's a lesson I learned as a teenager in The Boy Scouts that I was surprised to learn again as an adult in my flight attendant training. Whether I'm lost in the woods because I strayed away from my scout troop during a campout or because I'm a survivor in a plane that crashed in the wilderness, one initial piece of survival advice remains the same: *Sit down.*

When we're lost, hurt, or bewildered, our emotions are prone to running wild. Our minds can plummet towards panic. Our fears are vulnerable to hysteria. We're liable to do something harmful to ourselves. All of these factors can make us our own worst enemy.

That's why the experts who teach survival training tell us to do something simple yet highly helpful when we're disoriented and distraught – sit down and do nothing.

Earlier, I mentioned my high school reunion in Coffeyville, Kansas – the town where I grew up. Over the weekend, I paid a visit to "Mrs. Mary" (she and her husband sponsored our family to come to America; I addressed her by that name in error as a kid; I still address her by that name today, just for the heck of it). She's now elderly with grown children and quickly-growing grandchildren. While catching up on our family comings and goings over lunch, she related something that happened the prior week with her son that exemplifies this very topic.

"Gary" likes to take long hikes in the woods. One afternoon, he decided to go for a short hike and take a few things off his mind. Since he planned to be gone for only a brief time, he didn't take anything of substance with him, like food or water or extra clothing. About an hour into his hike, Gary discovered he must have been very preoccupied with the matters on his mind because he suddenly didn't know where he was. Confounded and dismayed, he had to admit he was completely lost. Not knowing where to go, Gary decided not to go anywhere. Instead, he sat down, did nothing for a while, then called for help on his cell phone.

The rescuers quickly arrived by helicopter. They provided the help Gary needed and also directed him to the spot where he parked his car – a spot that was only two miles away.

Although embarrassed that he was so close to his car, both Gary and his emergency rescuers know he did the right thing. If he hadn't sat down, collected himself, and called for help, he could have done something the rescuers have seen lots of people do – wander for miles in the wrong direction and turn a trivial coincidence into a terrible tragedy.

Both Gary and the responders knew when it was wise to move along and when it was even wiser to stay put. They knew that when our minds are in disarray, we tend to be up on our feet and moving around with our thoughts racing about. We're liable to be too frantic to think clearly. By sitting down, we force ourselves to take pause and push away the pangs of panic while gaining the clarity of thought. We induce a physical stillness that promotes a mental lucidity. We slow down our breathing and create a calm state of mind that fosters rational, productive thinking.

By sitting down and being neutral, we greatly improve our chances of getting out of our predicament, no worse for the wear (albeit with a tad of possible embarrassment).

~

I-I-I- . . . . s-s-t-t-u-t-t- . . . s-s-s-t-t-u-u-t-t-e-e-r-r-r.

Not all the time, but sometimes.

The cause of stuttering isn't exactly known. It's thought to be a psychological issue. It probably is with most people. For me though, it's more of a physical issue.

Sometimes, I have so many thoughts I want to express at once that I can't get them out as properly as I should. Sometimes, I try to articulate myself too fast. As a result, the words get clogged up in my mouth like debris getting clogged up in a funnel. When that happens, my body tenses up, and if the situation gets severe enough, I start to stutter.

76

Then one day, I noticed something. I noticed that my stuttering is tied to my physiological act of speaking.

When we talk, we naturally take in a breath of air and let it out as we say the words. Our diaphragm, the part of our torso that envelopes our lungs, inflates as we inhale, and deflates as we exhale.

I noticed that, with me, when I try to say the words too fast and the words get clogged up somewhere in the back of my throat, my diaphragm gets stuck in mid-exhale and the muscles around my torso constrict so tightly that I cannot breathe right and, subsequently, cannot get the words out right.

That's when I start to stutter.

Since noticing that, I worked out a remedy, one I wish I'd come up with much sooner. When the words get stuck in the vicinity of my tonsils, I take a slight pause and allow the constricting muscles around my diaphragm to relax. My body then loosens up, and that in turn loosens up my mind. Once my mind is at ease, I can let the words come trotting out of me in an orderly manner.

If I'm engaged in a long conversation, the stuttering will inevitably happen again during the conversation. That's when I remind myself to pause, do nothing for about 1.5 seconds, and let my torso muscles relax so that the words can take their time making an orderly exit.

~

Medically speaking, I wish the doctor who treated me when I was a teenager had known when it was best to do nothing. When I was about 15, my friends and I were sledding down "Big Hill" after a sizable snowfall. After many adventurous runs down the hill that night, we decided to go for one last hurrah before heading home. Three or four of us boys piled onto a sled and sped down the hill. About halfway down, the sled flipped over, tossing all of us every which way. Being the adventuresome kids that we were, we picked ourselves off the snow and had a good laugh at the tumble we took.

"That was fun!" my friends exclaimed. I excitedly agreed too, until I took a step with my right foot. That's when the pain hit me. That's when I knew something had gone wrong.

I went home that night, thinking my swollen ankle had suffered a minor sprain. Two days later, when the swelling hadn't subsided and the sharp pain hadn't gone away, I suspected that the injury was worse than I thought, that I had damaged a bone somehow, and I said so to my father. Upon hearing my concern, my father, being the immigrant that he was, took me to a chiropractor, thinking that a "doctor" who attended to the bones in a person's back was the appropriate doctor for a broken ankle.

The kindly chiropractor referred us to a medical doctor, and we went to a well-known physician in town. He took an x-ray, confirmed that my ankle was broken, and put it in a cast. Six weeks later, he removed my cast, pronounced my ankle as healed, and sent me on my way.

For months afterwards, the pain persisted. I chalked it up as a normal part of the healing process. After all, the well-known doctor in town said my ankle was good to go. Who was I to disagree?

Eventually, the pain did go away. I began walking around without any trouble from my ankle. Then a few years later, the pain came back. At the time, I was working at our restaurant in Winfield, Kansas for the summer. I was on my feet practically from dawn to dusk. Each day, the discomfort from my ankle would get a little worse. I disregarded the pain until it wouldn't let me disregard it any more.

I went to a doctor whose office was down the street from our restaurant. He took an x-ray and gave me the news. My ankle was still broken. I couldn't believe my ears. I told him the original doctor who treated me in Coffeyville, Kansas had pronounced my ankle as completely healed. He shook his head and said the current x-ray told a different story. I asked him what I could do to fix my ankle. Could I put it in a cast again and make it whole again? No, he answered. It's too late. The broken ends of the bone had calcified, causing a permanent non-union. If the original doctor had left my ankle in a cast a few more weeks, he said, then my ankle would have healed correctly. As it was, I now had a permanent, broken ankle.

That was about 30 years ago, and I've had to deal with my broken ankle ever since. Not a day goes by when the permanent discomfort makes me wish my original doctor had taken a neutral course of action towards my ankle. Everyday, I wish he had left my ankle in a cast for a few more weeks. I wish he had done nothing in that time frame and let my ankle heal as it should have.

Neutral Positioning

Neutral thinking can be more than a state of mind. It can also be a state of body, and the benefits of that physical manifestation can prove to be useful than in athletics . . . and beyond.

~

In basketball, where does the jump-ball take place to start a game? As I'm sure you know, it's not on one end of the court near one team's basket, nor is it on the other end of the court near the other team's basket. It's right in the middle where it's neutral and doesn't favor one team or the other.

The rule is the same for many other sports like soccer and hockey.

~

Have you ever noticed where professional tennis players stand when they're receiving serve? They don't stand way over to one side of the service box where they're vulnerable to a passing forehand, and they don't stand way over to the other side of the service box where they're vulnerable to a passing backhand. Nope, they position themselves towards the center of the service box where they can equally cover the forehand and backhand.

On a tangential note, I've enjoyed the game of tennis since high school. (Note that I said I've enjoyed the game, not that I'm good at it.) Like the majority of the human population, I'm right-handed. While goofing off on a tennis court one afternoon with some friends in college, I decided to switch hands and play with my left hand. I expected to be a real klutz at it, but to my utter surprise, I wasn't half bad. I actually hit some good shots with my foreign side. Encouraged, I kept playing with my left hand that afternoon, and many afternoons after that.

Today, I would say that my left-handed forehand is better than my right-handed forehand. (If you're tempted to argue that this is more of a commentary on how bad my right-handed forehand is, rather than how good my left-handed forehand is, you may have grounds for a valid assertion.) In any case, I wondered what else I could do left-handed, so I expanded my left-handed proclivity to the other aspects of my everyday life. I would have to say the results have been rewarding.

I can now write legibly with my left hand. It's an ability that came in handy when I needed to take copious notes in college and got tired of using my right hand. I can eat left-handed using a fork or spoon, although my ability with chopsticks still lacks an acceptable dexterity. I'm proud to say I can even tie my shoelaces left-handed. (If you're scoffing at that last one, don't be too quick to judge. When you tie your shoelaces left-handed, you have to reverse the order of the procedure, and it's not as simple as you might think. I didn't realize this until I actually tried it, and it took me awhile to get the gears in my brain to properly synchronize the steps in an orderly manner.)

The more I used my left hand, the more I realized I was balancing the two sides of my body. I was allowing my body to become neutral in its dependency on one particular side.

What's that, I hear you say?

How this can be of benefit?

Funny you should ask.

In sports, it has provided some definite advantages. If I'm playing a game of basketball and driving to the basket with a defender in front of me, I can increase my chances of scoring by utilizing my left hand. If the defender sees that I completely favor my right hand, he can devote his entire defense to my right-handed dribble. But if he sees that I can drive to the basket with my left hand too, then he has to split his defense. He has to cover my right-handed dribble *and* my left-handed dribble. By forcing him to divide his coverage between two opposing sides, I have doubled my chances of scoring on him.

By chance, do you play tennis yourself? Have you ever had to serve with the sun blaring brightly into your eyes? It's a real nuisance, isn't it? My answer to that is to utilize my ambidexterity. If I'm playing right-handed and find myself serving into the sun, I simply switch hands and serve left-handed. That way, I'm facing the other way and the sun isn't in my eyes anymore.

This aptitude to switch hands is dandy for casual sports, but does it make any real difference in the quality of one's life? Actually, it does stand to make a difference. Although in my case, I hope I never have to see the realization of that difference.

My father's side of the family has a history of high cholesterol and diabetes. These hereditary traits can threaten the onset of a stroke. Sadly for my Grandfather and uncle, those threats have come true. My Grandfather suffered a stroke in the latter part of his life. A few years after he passed away, my uncle succumbed to the same fate and suffered a debilitating stroke. Both were paralyzed. Both were bound to a wheelchair for more than a decade before they went to the grave. Both were right-handed. Both saw the usage of their right hand wither away. Neither were adept with their left hand because they never developed the dexterity in their left hand.

I hope to provide a different future for myself.

Although I have thus far dodged diabetes, I haven't been able to evade high cholesterol. Despite avidly exercising and maintaining a healthy diet (I swear I'm not a perpetual patron of McDonald's), my annual check-up consistently puts my cholesterol at a high level. While I continue to fight the fatty molecules in my bloodstream, I'll take comfort in knowing that I'll be as prepared as I can be if I should ever fall prey to a stroke. If that ailment ever gets a hold of me and renders my right hand useless, I will have the motor skills of my left hand all revved up and ready to go.

In football, where does the center typically place the ball to begin a play? Unless it's an unusual play of some sort that requires the ball to be way over on the left side of the field or way over on the right side of the field, he'll place the ball right in the middle where his team can optimize both sides of the field.

Speaking of football, I would be remiss in not mentioning that I had a brush with fame while I was in college at Oklahoma State University. I attended OSU at the same time Barry Sanders did. You've heard of him, right? The prolific running back who won the Heisman trophy then went on to achieve greatness in the NFL? Anyway, one of my part-time jobs at the time was working the concession stand at the local movie theatre. The college football team had a tradition where they went to the movies together the night before a home game. It was there at Carmike Cinemas that I made my claim to fame when I sold a popcorn and Coke to Barry, or as the school newspaper called him because of his modest persona, "Bashful Barry."

Admittedly, Barry wasn't the fastest running back in the history of the game. Nevertheless, he was in the top echelon because he was so productive, and it is my belief that he was so productive because he was so elusive. This was a fact to which many of his defenders could attest. To tackle him, they first had to catch him, but it was so hard to catch him because he was so adept at slipping through their fingers.

What was the quality that fueled Barry's elusiveness? I – and many others – would assert that it was his innate ability to make sudden, lateral movements.

When Barry moved laterally so quickly, he was – in essence – momentarily being neutral, even if only for a mercurial moment, even if only for a blink of an eye.

When he was "juking" this way and that way to evade his chasers, he often wasn't going forward or backwards. He was pausing in his progress, being neutral just for a nanosecond or two, before bursting forward to gain additional, crucial yardage.

That's right. Barry Sanders won the Heisman trophy and broke all sorts of professional football records by not doing anything for a fleeting moment or two. He did all of that by making neutral as part of his prowess. You don't have to take my word for it. Just watch his highlight reels and count the times when he went sideways just before he shot forward. Again and again, he made being neutral an integral part of his record-setting gains.

Just as I would be remiss in not mentioning my brush with Barry's fame at that movie theatre in Stillwater, OK – I would also be remiss in not bringing up a heart-to-heart conversation I had with him many years later. As it so happened, Barry was so taken with my excellent customer service skills at the concession stand that he promised me to keep in touch with me after he departed from OSU.

And he did.

Decades after we left the university and went our separate ways, the two of us met up again to compare the notes marking the milestones of our lives. By then, he'd been inducted into the NFL Hall Of Fame, and I had become a seasoned flight attendant. At an Ethiopian restaurant in Detroit, we enjoyed some intriguing cuisine. Somewhere between sampling the spicy bread and sipping the restaurant's sweet, herbal tea, I couldn't help notice that Barry was somewhat despondent. When I asked him what was the matter, he said it was nothing. Despite those words and his outward stoicism, it was obvious that something was indeed the matter. It took me a while to coax the truth out of him. Reluctantly, Bashful Barry finally confessed that while he was happy with achieving his stellar football career and obtaining financial riches beyond his dreams, he was somewhat dejected that he was never able to make one of his biggest dreams come true.

His admission took me totally by surprise. When I asked him what that dream was, I received another surprise. Barry said he'd always yearned to be a flight attendant and was downcast that he'd never been able to achieve that goal in his life. He said not being able to roam the skies on a jumbo jet had left a hole in his heart, a hole he didn't know if he could ever fill.

With a sympathetic sigh, I told him that not all of our dreams come true, that not everyone can become a flight attendant, and that he should take comfort in the accomplishments he'd attained and be content with that. I told him that he should revel in the fact that he won the Heisman trophy and that he was the envy of many men, young and old, who wished they could do what he did on the football field. Slowly, my message got through to him, and I was relieved to see that he brightened noticeably by the time the waiter brought us some steaming coffee to go with the sweet baklavas we were having for dessert. When we parted company for the night, I was gladdened to see that Barry had come to terms with not being able to achieve his life-long dream of becoming a flight attendant.

As I wind down this anecdote about Barry and me, I just have to add one more thing: *I sure hope you didn't believe the cockamamie story I just told you!*

It was a bunch of bologna, of course.

Not quite all of it, just most of it. Although I really did attend OSU when Barry won the Heisman trophy, and I really did sell him a Coke and popcorn at the local movie theatre, the rest of what I said was total hogwash.

You must have known that, right? Come on, Barry Sanders distraught about not becoming a flight attendant? If that's not knucklehead nonsense, I don't know what is.

But just in case you still want to believe there's an ounce of truth in that tall-tale yarn I just yanked you around with, then I would like to sell you miles and miles of prime, tropical real estate in the Sahara Desert that's filled with lush, abundant greenery.

~

How about a do-nothing activity that's good for the body *and* mind?

You do it everyday. It's called "sleep."

Heck, since you're reading my book, you might be doing it right now. Yep, I admit it. My writing has been known to put some people to sleep. It's not exactly a quality I strive for, but if I can cure someone of their insomnia, I don't mind doing my part to improve their well-being. When I'm not helping out society in this way, I'm discovering that by lying down and going to sleep, I'm literally helping my body get back into a natural, balanced state.

Not too long ago, I had traveled to Dubai in the United Arab Emirates. On my way home, I ran into some unexpected snags that severely extended my travel time. For almost two days, I was either sitting or standing while catching only a few winks on the fly – literally. By the time I got home, my legs had been in a vertical position for so long that my feet were significantly swollen due to my bodily fluids pooling down at my feet. It wasn't until I went to bed, placed my body in a horizontal position, and slept soundly for about 12 hours that the fluids were able redistribute evenly throughout my body and take the swelling away.

I'm sure you've had your moments of sleeplessness. It's during those times that you become acutely aware of how vital sleep is to our human body, not just physically but also mentally too. By closing our eyes and letting ourselves enter a subconscious state and doing nothing for about 8 hours, we provide a means for our body to recharge and our mind to refresh, all while lying prone and investing in the neutral state of sleep.

Sadly, some people suffer from excessive insomnia and can't get the sleep they desperately need. Again, this is where my innate skills can be of use. If you know anyone who's in need of a good snooze, be a kind soul. Give them a copy of my book, and there's a good chance they'll be snoring before they can finish page 1.

Some More Fence Sitting

Chances are that you've heard some jokes about Swiss neutrality. Perhaps you've even told a few of those jokes yourself. Most likely, you're only familiar with the outer coating of this perception. That's how I was until I looked beyond the façade. The more I looked, the more I realized how undeserving it is.

True, Switzerland was neutral during World War II. As was the case with many other countries at that time, it did what it had to do to protect its salvation.

Is that so bad?

Would you be a bad person if you acted to protect your salvation?

A quick glance at a map will tell us that Switzerland is a landlocked country – a meatball on the tines of many forks, if you will – vulnerable to attack from a number of powerful countries, notably Nazi Germany. When the Second World War broke out, Switzerland declared itself neutral to steer clear of the coming destruction. Essentially, it was sticking up for itself to save itself.

Again, is that so bad?

If your answer is Yes, then let's personalize this matter. If someone is being threatened with harm, doesn't that person have the right to do what it takes to save herself? If she doesn't act in her own best interest, who will?

In case that depiction didn't work for you, let's try another one. If you're walking down the street and happen to come upon a robbery in progress, and you see that the victim is about to get shot, would you throw yourself in front of that person to take the bullet for him? Would you die for a total stranger? If your answer is Yes, then you deserve a great round of altruistic applause. If your answer is No, then do you automatically deserve condemnation? Are you fair game for moral castigation?

Every nation has a right to look out for itself, including The United States Of America – which was why America stayed out of WW II for two years until the bayonet of war forced it into action.

Contrary to what many Americans think, WW II didn't start in 1941. It started in 1939. America didn't see fit to enter the war until 1941 when Japan bombed Pearl Harbor. Up to then, America was content to stay neutral in order to serve its own best interest. Should America be criticized for acting in its own best interest?

Heck, no.

And neither should Switzerland, especially since quite a bit of good did come about as a result of its neutrality.

Hundreds of thousands of refugees from the surrounding countries, for example, were able to find shelter in Switzerland because it was neutral. Among those hundreds of thousands of refugees were tens of thousands of Jewish people fleeing the Nazi wrath. Without Switzerland to serve as their haven, they would have likely perished along with their countrymen who couldn't find any kind of sanctuary from the genocidal storm.

~

"We interrupt this message to inform you that the Ebola virus has come to a neighborhood near you!"

Although that wasn't the actual message that we heard, it might as well have been. It was the autumn of 2014, and the deadly Ebola virus had come to the forefront of America's everyday life. One person who had flown from Africa to Dallas, TX died from the virus. Shortly after he perished, one of the nurses who cared for him learned she had also contracted the disease. Days after that, another nurse who cared for him learned she had also been infected with the virus. Worse, the second nurse then boarded a plane and potentially infected hundreds of other people. The fear was that those people would infect hundreds of other people, and those hundreds of people would infect thousands of other people, and those thousands people would infect . . .

Exponential contagion was the fear, and the fear was exponentially contagious.

During a typical flight, it's common for the pilots to get on the radio and chit-chat with the staff on the ground. On a flight I was working at this time, the captain told us flight attendants that a member of the ground staff had told him that a flight from New York City to Los Angeles was quarantined because a passenger onboard had been diagnosed with Ebola virus. Naturally, all of us crewmembers became very concerned. Some of the comments and questions that we tossed back and forth between ourselves included:

- Since that plane was bound for L.A., that means the flight attendants onboard are based in L.A. Since we're also based in L. A., that means the flight attendants on that plane could be our friends and acquaintances. What's going to happen to them?
- Where would the authorities put the plane while it's in quarantine? In a hangar? And would all the passengers and crewmembers have to stay onboard the plane during the quarantine?
- What about the flight that we're working right now? Could someone on our plane have the Ebola virus too?
- If we catch the virus without knowing it, could we bring it home and give it to our friends and families?

Our discussion became animated with even more questions and concerns, but fortunately, discuss was all we did. We didn't let our fears manifest into adverse actions. We didn't panic. Instead, we decided that it was too soon to arrive at any conclusions and that it was best to wait until we landed in Los Angeles to get the full story.

A few hours later, we landed in L. A. as scheduled and contacted a couple of reliable sources at our base. To our relief, the story we received was that there was no story. The staff member on the ground who had told the captain that one of our planes from New York City had been quarantined was perpetuating a bad rumor. Upon confirming the fabrication of the account, we flight attendants were glad we maintained a neutral frame of mind and didn't give in to any erratic actions.

Neutral and Calm

Being neutral induces a calmness.
Being calm induces a lucidity.
Being lucid induces a wisdom.

There have been times when I wasn't calm, lucid, or wise, so it's a good thing there were others around me who were. One instance that comes to mind involves a trek to Machu Pichu in Peru.

Onward and Upward to Machu Pichu – part 1

Machu Pichu had been on my list of places to go for a number of years. I'd wanted to go in March of 2011, but my friend Ingrid who lives in Peru said to hold off because the excessive rains that spring had made travel to the historical site difficult. I listened and waited. During my wait, I happened to mention my travel aspiration to Kimberly, my friend in Los Angeles. Right away, she said she wanted to join me on my trip. I told her, "Sure. The more, the merrier."

By the month of May, the rains had yielded to sunshine, giving Kimberly and me the green light to head for Peru. We flew out of L.A. and stopped over in Houston. Since we had lengthy wait before our flight to Lima, we kicked back in the airline lounge where Kimberly was a member and indulged ourselves in a few complimentary margaritas. After one . . . then three drinks – no, two drinks – no . . . four . . . or was it three . . . something like that . . . I remembered how I had a low tolerance for alcohol and cut myself off at 3 margaritas . . . or so.

The six-hour flight to Lima gave me ample time to sleep off the alcoholic drinks. We arrived around midnight, and our connecting flight to Cusco didn't depart until 6 a.m. With some time to while away, we pushed together some chairs, arranged them side by side, and pretended that the makeshift benches was just like cushy lounge chairs that coddled us in Houston.

Kimberly didn't care much for her bumpy bench. I didn't mind it really. I'd slept in a urine-drenched hotel room in Africa. I'd battled humongous mosquitoes in Cambodia. I'd ridden in crowded buses for hours on end in Vietnam. Obstacles on the road were an adventurous part of travel as far as I was concerned, and when it came to adventure, I'm not terribly shy about stepping up and asking for more.

While my bumpy accommodation was tolerable, the long wait in the transit area wasn't. The hours ambled by like a gluttonous man making his tenth trip to the all-you-can-eat buffet bar. When it finally came time to check in for our flight to Cusco, Kimberly and I were both sleepless and fatigued. We trudged up to the check-in line and joined the crowd gathered at the gate. The fray around us was distracting yet not alienating. I had never been to Peru before, and as was the case when I'm in a new country, I was too busy absorbing the novelty of the sights and sounds to be bothered by anything else.

When the boarding commenced, Kimberly and I handed our paper tickets to the gate agent and received our boarding passes in return. We then filed onto the plane and looked for our seats. As it so happened, the two of us were in the front row of Coach. We sat down, closed our eyes, and began to sip from the quenching glass of sleep, not realizing that the placement of our seats was the perfect stage for the upcoming scene of vexing drama.

As a flight attendant, I'm used to working odd hours. I'm used to forcing myself to be awake when I want to be asleep. The lack of slumber from the long wait in the transit area wasn't troubling. I was more concerned about the effects of the altitude in Cusco. I'd read how the high altitude of that city could make breathing difficult. I'd read how it could make people nauseous. I'd wondered how the lack of oxygen would affect my companion and me.

Before I could delve much into that worry, something else happened to occupy my mind.

"Excuse me, Mr. Dao," I heard somebody say. The words prodded me out of the dreamland I was wandering into. I opened my eyes and saw a gate agent peering down at me. He was friendly, smiling, and his name badge read, "Alberto."

"Yes?" I groggily replied.

"Do you have your ticket?" he asked me in a thick accent.

"My ticket?"

"Yes, your ticket. Can I see it?"

I didn't have my ticket. I gave it to one of the gate agents in exchange for my boarding pass. I gathered Alberto must have meant my boarding pass, so I pulled it out of my pocket and showed it to him.

"No," Alberto said upon seeing what I had produced. "That's your boarding pass. I need your ticket."

Before I became a flight attendant, I worked as a ticket agent. I very well knew the difference between a ticket and a boarding pass. "I understand what you're saying," I told Alberto, "but I don't have my ticket. I gave it to you guys when I boarded the plane. That's how I got my boarding pass."

"You don't have your ticket?" Alberto asked me again.

"No," I confirmed.

With his smile still in place, Alberto chirped, "Okay. Thank you," and walked out the front door, rattling off something to somebody on the other end of his walkie-talkie radio.

"That was weird," Kimberly muttered, grogginess weighing down her voice.

"Yeah, it was," I mumbled in agreement.

Whatever misunderstanding had produced that exchange, it was over with as far as I was concerned. Both Kimberly and I sat back, closed our eyes, and picked up where we left off in our venture into dreamland.

Five minutes later, just was I was about to go for a swim in one of Dreamland's serene lakes, another "Excuse me, Mr. Dao" prodded me awake.

I opened my eyes. Alberto was back, smiling contritely. "Yes?" I answered.

"Are you sure you don't have your ticket?"

With some effort, I kept my irritation out of my voice. "Yes, I'm sure," I told him without any uncertainty.

"I'm sorry to bother you. We can't find your ticket. Can you check your pockets again?"

I knew without a doubt that I didn't still have my ticket. To appease him, however, I stood up and checked my front and back pockets. "See?" I told Alberto when I proved to him that the ticket wasn't in my pockets. "I don't have the ticket."

"Can you check your bag too?" he inquired.

The look I gave him was incredulous. His sheepish smile told me he was catching a whiff of my irritation. "Please?" he practically peeped.

To appease him yet again, I opened the overhead bin above my seat and searched through my bag. As expected, the ticket wasn't there. I turned and said as much to Alberto, all the while wondering if he would ask me if *he* could look through my bag too. Fortunately – and unfortunately – he didn't.

I say "fortunately" because he would have stepped across the line of proper decorum if he'd asked me if he could rummage through my bag too.

I say "unfortunately" because if he had searched my bag, he might have been satisfied with the results and might not have done what he did next.

"Thank you, Mr. Dao," Alberto said before he again walked away, chattering into his walkie-talkie.

I sat down. Kimberly looked at me quizzically and said, "Okay, that was *really* weird."

"Tell me about it," I answered. "How many times do I have to tell the guy I don't have my ticket?"

Apparently, twice was not enough.

Minutes later, as I was settling down on the homestead I'd mapped out in my vast Dreamland, Alberto came back for another round of our newfound game called: *Where's your ticket, Mr. Dao?*

"Um, excuse me," Alberto said with reluctance.

I opened my eyes and regarded my newly-minted tormentor. "Yes?"

"Are you sure you don't have your ticket?"

I took a deep breath, laboring to suppress my disbelief. "Yes, I'm sure," I answered, then unwilling and unable to contain my annoyance any further, I proceeded to tell him what he should have known already: "I had to give you guys my ticket before you would give me my boarding pass. The fact that I have my boarding pass means I gave you my ticket. If you lost my ticket, that's your fault, not mine. Stop asking me if I still have my ticket!"

Alberto's sheepish smile turned into outright embarrassment. "I'm sorry, but we can't find your ticket. You have to get off the plane until we do."

I couldn't believe what I was hearing and had to repeat it for confirmation. "I have to get off the plane until you find my ticket?"

"Yes."

"That's not right," I objected, feeling like I'd just been ejected into a jungle filled with ensnaring vines. "Besides, the plane is about to leave."

"Yes, the plane will leave. You will stay," he said matter-of-factly.

A trap door in the jungle overgrown with vicious vines fell open and dropped me into the pond of justifiably pissed off. "Let me get this straight," I began. "I give you guys my ticket. You lose it, and now you're going to kick me off the plane until you find it."

"Yes," Alberto confirmed.

I paused for a moment to try and calm myself. It didn't work. "No way!" I told him. "If you guys lost my ticket, that's your problem, not mine!"

Alberto sighed and spoke into his walkie-talkie – only to have the person on the other end of it bark back his command. Their dialogue was all in Spanish and completely incomprehensible to me. Alberto must have noticed that because he dutifully relayed the message to me in English: "My supervisor says you have to get off the plane, Mr. Dao."

Obviously, my eviction notice wasn't Alberto's brainchild, especially since everyone on the plane had become our audience – notably an American couple sitting across the aisle from Kimberly and me – and the sight of our spectacle was making Alberto more than a bit uncomfortable. It was his supervisor who was behind this ridiculous scheme. If that was the case, I surmised, then it would only be appropriate if I talked to the supervisor himself. "If your supervisor wants to kick me out," I stated to the messenger in front of me, "then I would like to talk to him in person."

Alberto conveyed my wishes into the walkie-talkie. The reply that shot back was heated and hostile. Apparently, the supervisor was pissed off that I was pissed off. As Alberto turned a shade of red that would have made a beet turn green with envy, he informed me, "My supervisor said you can talk to him after you step off the plane. It's departure time."

Before I could protest again, the couple across the aisle intervened on my behalf. "Hey, listen," the husband told Alberto. "This Mr. Dao guy is right. He has that boarding pass because he gave you his ticket. If you lost the ticket, that's your fault, not his."

"Yeah, you can't kick him off the plane!" the wife tossed in.

"I'm sorry," Alberto told my intervening benefactors, "but he has to get off the plane." He turned to me and repeated, "You have to get off the plane."

My mind and my ears were still having a disconnect. This unseen supervisor of Alberto's wanted to kick me off the plane because they lost my ticket. In my book, that made about as much sense as saying $2 + 2 = 5$. "Your supervisor isn't making any sense," I told Alberto. "If he wants to kick me off the plane, I would like him to come onboard and tell me that himself."

The look on Alberto's face said he wished he'd taken the day off and gone fishing. Against his druthers, he forwarded my message to his supervisor, and in return, he got what could only be construed as a blaring, Spanish equivalent of: "WHAT DO YOU MEAN THAT GUY WANTS TO TALK TO ME IN PERSON! I SAID GET HIS ASS OFF THE PLANE! YOU GET HIS ASS OFF THE PLANE – NOW!" If beet red was a bad color for Alberto, crimson red suited him worse. In a voice that was more tepid than lukewarm water, Alberto said to me, "My supervisor wants you to get off the plane right away."

The scene we were causing wasn't embarrassing only for Alberto. It was undeniably unsettling for me as well. I pride myself on respecting the locals wherever I go. At the moment, rightfully or not, I was being about as disrespectful as can be. With all the commotion I was stirring up, I wondered if it wouldn't be a bad idea for me to go along with the supervisor's demand. Then another thought occurred to me. I wondered what would happen if I did get off the plane and they couldn't find my ticket. "Um," I posed to Alberto, "what happens if I get off and you can't find my ticket?"

Alberto shrugged with indifference. "Then you buy a new one."

What! I yelled in my mind. *You mean I would be buying two tickets for the same flight? Oh, no! There's no way I'm gonna do that!*

With this new development, the eardrums in my head were beating out the alarm that yelled: "CAUTION! SCAM AHEAD!"

I'd heard how some airlines in South America blatantly ripped people off. One such story came from a friend who said while she was waiting in line to check in for her flight, one of the airline representatives came out and announced to all the passengers that whoever wanted to secure a seat would have to come to the front of the line and pay an extra fee, and that whoever didn't pay the extra fee would risk not getting on the flight because all the seats would be gone by the time they reached the counter. I wondered if this was such a scam, only better disguised.

I didn't know. More importantly, I didn't care. There was no way I was going to pay for two tickets for the same flight!

"Get me get this straight," I told Alberto. "You lost my ticket, and if you can't find that so-called lost ticket, I have to buy a new one?"

"Yes," he confirmed with an oddly sincere smile.

Up until now, I couldn't believe my ears. Now I couldn't believe my eyes. Judging by the innocent smile on Alberto's face, he truly didn't comprehend the hidden context of what he was saying – that his supervisor was most likely fabricating a "lost" ticket story so he could force me to buy a new one. As a matter of fact, if this unseen supervisor could somehow get me off the plane and out to the ticket counter, I could already see him telling me I had to pay for the new ticket with cash to make the transaction more "convenient," and as soon as I turned away, he would sneak the cash into his pocket. I didn't intend to let that happen.

"I'm not buying two tickets!" I told Alberto flat out. "If you really lost my ticket, you deal with it!"

Out of nowhere, another question popped into my head, and it had to do with my checked bag. "If I got off the plane," I asked Alberto, "what would happen to the bag that I checked in already?

Without a beat, he answered, "It will go without you."

Aw, hell no! I wanted to shout out loud. *You're going to send my bag ahead of me to Cusco and hold it hostage there to give me an even bigger incentive to buy another ticket? Aw, hell no!*

"That's not right!" I told him. "You can't send my bag off without me and force me to go after it!"

Alberto poured my message into his walkie-talkie. The reply that blasted back from the supervisor was harsh and heavy. Wincing from the impact, Alberto turned to me and practically begged me to do as his superior said: "You have to get off the plane!"

The supervisor's barbed tone did nothing to allay my rampant annoyance. Unfortunately, I had to go through Alberto to deliver my message. Sternly, I said to Alberto, "Or what?"

He wisely didn't pick up the gauntlet I threw down. Instead, he passed it to the man on the other end of the walkie-talkie. As expected, the reply boomeranged right back. Apparently, the supervisor didn't think his messenger was capable of getting the job done himself. It was time for the off-site king to call in his muscle: *Security!*

The security guy – "Butch" I'll call him – came bounding in the door. He came up to Alberto and mumbled something to him. Alberto apprised Butch of the stand-off. Butch turned his eyes to me and began looking me up and down, probably sizing me up to see if it would be best to grab me by the arms or the legs when he commenced to drag me kicking and screaming from the plane.

If push came to shove, and if we'd been in the good ole U.S. of A., that's exactly what Butch would have had to do to get me off the plane – drag me kicking and screaming! As it was, we weren't in the good ole U.S. of A. We were in Peru, a country whose justice system was a complete unknown to me. *What was the Peruvian penalty for refusing to get off the plane?* 10 years in prison? 20 lashes in the middle of the city square? A lifetime of scrubbing all the airplane lavatories? Obviously, I wasn't getting a fair shake at the moment, but there are plenty of justice systems around the world where "fair" is laughable word. Plus, there was Kimberly to think of. If I went down fighting, what would happen to her?

I leaned over and asked my companion, "What do you want to do?" Secretly, I was hoping she would cry out, "Remember the Alamo! Let's fight these dirty bastards to the bitter end!" Fortunately for the both of us, she didn't.

Kimberly considered my question for a couple of seconds before coming to her conclusion. Calmly, she said, "Let's go along with them for now and see what happens."

Although it wasn't the option I was hoping for, it was an option I could live with. Resignedly, I got out of my seat. Kimberly did the same. I opened the overhead bin to retrieve my carry-on bag, begrudgingly going along with the airline staff's ridiculous edict . . . when a miracle happened!

Another gate agent, a young lady who was an angel rising to crush the conniving scheme of the devils around her, came running up the aisle from the back entrance, huffing and puffing. Excited and exasperated, she announced to me: "We found your ticket! We found your ticket!"

Apparently, she had been listening to the whole ordeal on her radio and decided enough was enough. From what I can surmise, she could see that the verbal altercation was nearing a physical altercation – and against her colleague's wishes – she didn't want to risk a chance of fisticuffs.

Flabbergasted, I looked on as she held up my ticket – the one that I had indeed handed to the gate agents in order to get my boarding pass. Vindicated, I slowly turned to Alberto.

"Looks like you guys found my lost ticket after all," I seethed, not bothering to mop up the acidic sarcasm dripping from my words.

Alberto's retreat was abrupt and unadulterated. "Sorry! You can go! Bye!" Faster than you can say – *The gig is up!* – all the airline agents on that plane spun around and bolted out the front door.

Kimberly and I sat down, dazed and amazed that such a bizarre event had taken place, and that it had come to a conclusion so suddenly.

"I can't believe that just happened," Kimberly thought out loud.

"Me neither," I agreed in astonishment.

The plane took off – with me still in it – and we landed in Cusco an hour later.

While waiting for our bags at the luggage carousel, I replayed the event over and over in my mind, partly in disbelief that such a strange episode had occurred, partly glad that Kimberly was around to advise a calmer course of action. If she wasn't there, I might have been so foolish as to take up Butch on his offer to drag me off the plane kicking and screaming (and maybe with some feisty fists swinging wildly too.)

Still lost in thought, I looked up from the carousel and saw an unexpected sight: *All the passengers around the carousel weren't looking at the conveyer belt to keep an eye out for their bags; instead, everyone was looking at me, regarding me with a sense of dismay and wariness.*

I was baffled as to why I had become their main attraction. About 1.5 seconds later, the realization hit me.

A good number of the passengers who witnessed my front-row incident on the plane spoke only Spanish and couldn't understand everything I was saying to Alberto. Moreover, even if they spoke English, they might have been too far back from the commotion to hear everything that was said. In all likelihood, most of them only saw me arguing extensively with Alberto – engaging in a prolonged, heated exchange. Added to that was the spectacle of a security guy coming onboard to drag me off the plane. Mostly likely, they didn't hear my version of the story which was: *"Hey, ho! I gave you my ticket, so let me go!"*

Since most of them didn't hear or didn't completely comprehend the incident that transpired, they probably thought I was some sort of troublemaker who was raising hell and concluded it was a good idea to steer clear of me. I took in all the bewildered eyes resting on me and became amused at the misinterpretation. For a moment, I was tempted to stick out my chest, thump it a few times (Tarzan-style, of course) and bellow with overly pompous pride: "That's right! I'm a bad-ass! Anybody else want a piece of me and my so-called lost ticket!"

Of course, I didn't do any such thing. I simply waited for my bag to come out. When it did, I removed it from the carousel and followed Kimberly out of baggage claim. We caught a taxi and proceeded to the hotel. On the way there, I was glad I wasn't evicted from the plane. I was happy to be in Cusco and on my way to Machu Pichu. I was thanking my lucky stars that the rest of the trip would be free of any controversy. Within 72 hours, I would discover I was thanking the wrong stars.

Onward and Upward to Machu Pichu – part 2

My heart was beating like a tom-tom drum that was feverishly signaling an imminent enemy attack. It kept racing, and thudding, and pounding – not allowing me to get a wink of sleep.

I recognized the symptoms. I knew what was happening. I had tried to prepare myself for it. The preparation didn't do me any good.

It was oxygen deprivation, a condition that could lead to altitude sickness. Although I wasn't in any immediate danger of becoming stricken with the illness, I knew I was getting a small sampling of its effects, and that made me wary of what else I might be getting a sampling of.

Cusco is more than two miles above sea level. When you're that much closer to outer space, you're getting that much less oxygen. Consequently, your heart will beat that much faster to take in the oxygen that you need. It was a fact I was experiencing firsthand because, at that moment, my heart was doing its darndest to get me more of that precious O_2 molecule.

Kimberly and I had checked into our hotel. Upon entering the establishment, we were pleasantly surprised with the interior of the place. Too often, what you see on the internet is not what you get in person. With this hotel, we got what we saw. The front entrance had a security gate. Inside the gate was a reception desk, and between the reception desk and the stairs that led up to the rooms was a cozy dining area.

With our keys in hand, we climbed the one flight of stairs. Right away, I caught wind of the altitude sickness I'd only read about. After just one short flight of stairs, I was huffing and puffing like I'd just ran up five flights of stairs with a boulder on my back. Thankfully, my room was the first one at the top of the stairs. Kimberly's was at the end of the hallway. As soon as I reached my room, I paused and took a deep breath. When my breathing had regained a semblance of normalcy, I told Kimberly I would knock on her door in a few hours after I got in a good nap. She mumbled a fatigued, "Okay," and went to her room.

I entered my room, showered to scrub away the previous day's grime, and tumbled into bed. With the portable heater turned on and two blankets on top of me to ward off the chill in the early morning air, I closed my eyes and waited for sleep to find me.

Sleep must have gotten the wrong directions to my hotel room because I waited with great frustration for that valuable commodity to arrive. Thirty minutes lumbered by. Then another thirty minutes came and went. Then another hour. After that, another hour. I kept waiting and waiting.

More than three hours later, sleep was nowhere to be found. I began to wonder if sleep was a guy to who had gotten lost but was too macho to stop and ask for directions. If so, then the Peruvian version of the sandman wouldn't be finding me any time soon.

With growing discouragement, I kept lying there, contorted in my bed, listening to the thudding of my heart as it pounded away in its search for an ounce of oxygenated air.

Resistance was futile. I gave up on my search for sleep and wandered back into the land of the awake. I stepped into the bathroom, made myself publicly presentable, and went to Kimberly's room to see if she was as sleepless as I was.

I had expected to hear her say that she was. Imagine my surprise when she answered her door still rubbing the slumber out of her eyes. Clearly, the sandman didn't have any trouble finding Kimberly's room. As we made some quick arrangements to meet downstairs, it flitted through my mind that perhaps the sandman was a sexist provider who wouldn't give another guy the time of day but wouldn't hesitate to dote on a lovely lady.

About half an hour later, Kimberly and I sat down with the hotel's designated tour guide to discuss our venture to Machu Pichu. The tour he mapped out for us was one of the more popular ones. We would start out early the next morning to go to Aguas Caliente, the town at the base of Machu Pichu. Along the way – by way of bus and train – we would stop to see a couple of other sights before reaching Aguas Caliente late at night. We would stay in a hotel there overnight, get up early the next morning, go see Machu Pichu with a local tour guide, and then take the train back to Poroy where we would catch a taxi for the short ride to Cusco.

The price that the tour guide quoted was reasonable. We agreed. He asked for a deposit. We paid it.

Kimberly and I then strolled around Cusco for the rest of the day, absorbing the sights and sounds of the small city. At Plaza de Armas, the town's main square about half a mile from our hotel, we ran into the American couple who sat across the aisle from us on the plane. All of us laughed when we reflected on the transgression that occurred earlier that morning. I laughed especially hard when the wife of the couple said that if Butch had gone ahead and tried to drag me off the plane, she would have grabbed me by the feet and pulled me back I order to keep me on the plane. I told her it was good to know that she had my back.

After a few pictures of the surrounding scenery, Kimberly and I bid adios to the couple from the plane and meandered out of the square into some of the smaller streets. We passed by many restaurants displaying colorful pictures of a popular dish in Peru. While the photos of the dish were colorful in that they mixed in some vibrant colors, the subject repeatedly featured in the pictures was far from attractive. As a matter of fact, it was borderline grotesque.

The subject on display was that of a roasted guinea pig, disfigured head and all.

Meats sold in many markets typically don't have the heads still attached, most likely because people don't want to be able to identify the animal that had to die in order to become their evening entrée. I think there's a lot of truth in the claim that if people had to kill the animals they ate, there would be a lot more vegetarians amongst us.

In my travels, I'd been to plenty of markets in foreign countries where the heads of the animals were still attached to the bodies. Furthermore, as a boy who grew up on a farm in Kansas, I'd done my share of butchering where I removed the heads of the animals myself. Looking at the pictures we came across in Cusco, it wasn't the identifying aspect of it that bothered me. It was the potentially inhumane part that I found troublesome.

When I induced the demise of the animals on the farm, sending them to the "Great Farm In The Sky," I did it as an act of necessity and completed it succinctly. In regards to the butchered animals that I came across in foreign countries, I observed that they were expressionless which wasn't surprising since dead animals tend not to have expressions. The pictures of the guinea pig in Cusco proved to be the contrary. In those pictures, the ones that were supposed to make the potential diners salivate with hunger, the sight of the dead animal only made me queasy with discomfort.

The photos showed a guinea pig skinned, gutted, and charbroiled to the point where the mouth was pulled back into a, painful, teeth-baring grimace that made me want to inquire if the animal's life was mercifully quelled, or if it suffered unnecessarily when it met its death.

Fortunately for Kimberly and me, there were other discoveries to be made during our stroll through Cusco that didn't bear the mark of the macabre. At some point in the middle of the afternoon, we walked past a bakery. The cakes and pastries set out for display in the window were so delectable that we had to pop in to see if the beckoning delights tasted as good as they appeared.

The cozy shop afforded us a small table in the corner. Since our knowledge of Spanish was next to non-existent, we ordered using the most popular international language of all – pointing. We succeeded in relaying to the waitress the dishes we wanted to sample, a task that wasn't difficult since all we had to do was point to the appetizing arrangements in the window. For the drinks, Kimberly stuck with her bottle of water while I used my rudimentary Spanish to eke out an order of coffee with milk.

While we waited for our sweet snacks to arrive, we noticed there was a small flask containing a dark, brown liquid sitting in the middle of the table. Personally, I thought it was a small bottle of soy sauce. Kimberly said it couldn't be soy sauce because what would soy sauce be doing in a pastry shop? She had a point. I couldn't picture anyone sprinkling a dash of soy sauce onto their cupcake to make it more tasty. To satisfy my curiosity, I lifted the lid and took a quick whiff of the liquid. Kimberly was right. It wasn't soy sauce at all. It was coffee.

"Coffee!" Kimberly exclaimed in reaction to my statement.

Why would a pastry shop have coffee on the table as a condiment? we both wondered.

The answer arrived with our order.

The waitress placed Kimberly's pastry in front of her and my piece of cake in front of me. Then she placed a mug of warm milk down next to my cake. I thought there was some sort of misunderstanding. I had ordered coffee with milk, not milk only. "Excuse me," I said to the waitress while pointing to the mug of milk. "Café con leche?"

"Si," she replied courteously. "Café con leche."

This is my coffee with milk? I can see the milk part, but where's the coffee? Since I didn't know how to ask all that in Spanish, I proceeded slowly in English to better improve my chances of being understood. "I ordered coffee with milk. This is only milk."

With a patient smile, the waitress gave the flask of coffee on the table a little tap and said, "Café," then pointed to the mug of milk and said, "con leche."

The revelation hit Kimberly and me simultaneously, making us laugh out loud. Apparently, when you're in the States and order coffee with milk, you get a cup of coffee with a little bit of milk in it, but when you're in Peru and you order coffee with milk, you get a mug of *milk* with a little bit of *coffee* in it.

Afterwards, my companion and I explored more of Cusco's unheralded streets. When dusk started to set in, we headed back to the town square and took a gander at all the restaurants around us, wondering which one we should patronize for our evening meal. We finally settled on a restaurant with an inviting exterior and enjoyed our dinner at a table that provided a great view of the entire square. Sated, we returned to the hotel and turned in early. Tomorrow was going to require an early start, and we wanted to be well rested before setting off for Machu Pichu.

Settling into my bed, I was afraid that I would find sleep to be as elusive as I had that morning. Fortunately, I didn't. As I slipped beneath my covers, my beating heart was thankfully ticking along instead of thudding thunderously. It could have been that I had acclimated to the altitude. I didn't know. I didn't care. I just knew that when I closed my eyes, I enjoyed a good night's rest that allowed me to greet the next day's dawn with robust anticipation.

Seconds after I showered and shaved, the phone rang. It was Kimberly. She was asking me if I could spare the plastic laundry bag that came with each room. I glanced at the folded bag sitting on my closet shelf. "Yeah, you can have it," I told her, at the same time wondering how much dirty laundry she could have accumulated when we'd been in town for only one day. Jokingly, I asked her, "Have you gone through ten wardrobes already?"

Her groggy reply was leaden with exhaustion: "No, I've been throwing up all night. I used up my laundry bag. I'm gonna need yours for our trip today."

I could scarcely believe my ears. "You've been throwing up all night?"

"Yeah, I've got a bad headache too."

Vomiting and a bad headache! If those weren't symptoms of altitude sickness, I didn't know what was. "I'll be right over," I told her. I got dressed, grabbed my unused laundry bag, and hurried to Kimberly's room.

She answered the door looking like a bird that had been flogged and rendered flightless. "Morning," she groaned, noticeably leaving out the "Good" part of the greeting.

"Hi," I replied while she turned around and dragged herself back to her bed. I looked on and watched her crawl under her covers, apparently not having enough strength to sit up while talking to me. "You've been vomiting, and you have a bad headache?" I asked her to make sure I had the facts right.

"Yes," she sniffled with her eyes closed.

I placed my laundry bag on her nightstand. "Here's the bag," I said. "Can I get you anything else?"

"No, thanks."

As much as I knew she wanted some peace and quiet to get some rest, I had to ask her the question pressing on my mind: "Do you think you have altitude sickness?"

"It's either that or the bright moon that was shining down through my sky roof," she lamented. "It was so bright last night, I couldn't get any sleep. I think that's what gave me the headache and vomiting."

I looked up and saw that her room did indeed have a sky roof. The large glass panel was currently allowing the morning sun to saunter in without an invitation. Apparently, it had let in a lot of unwanted moonlight the night before as well. "Do you want an eye mask?" I asked Kimberly, referring to the elastic blinders that can be of great help when trying to get some sleep during the day. "I've got one in my bag," I offered.

"I've got one too. It didn't help."

I wasn't surprised to hear that Kimberly had an eye mask herself. Like me, she spent a lot of time on airplanes and knew that an eye mask and a pair of ear plugs were crucial to shutting out the unwanted sights and sounds to get some rest.

Kimberly turned towards me. "What time does our tour start this morning?"

Oh, yes. The tour. I'd forgotten about that. "Um," I said, glancing at my watch, "I think the guide is going to meet us downstairs in about an hour."

A weary moan trickled out of her. "I don't think I can make it," she admitted with her eyes closed.

I counted the hours in store for us that morning. The excursion would start with a long bus ride all morning followed by an extensive train ride all afternoon that would get us into Aguas Caliente around midnight. I had to agree with Kimberly's assessment. It wouldn't be good to have her sick and vomiting all the way to Aguas Caliente. While I was thinking all this over, I glanced up at the sky roof and was baffled as to how the moonlight could have caused such an intense reaction in Kimberly. Plus, she'd tried the eye mask and found that useless. Personally, whenever I put on an eye mask, I was immediately submerged in a restful setting of pitch black darkness. All in all, I thought Kimberly was having a classic case of altitude sickness. Whatever the situation actually was, the consequence was the same: *Kimberly was ill and in no condition to hit the road.* It was best for us to stay put. "All right," I told her. "You take it easy and I'll go talk to the guide."

"Okay," Kimberly said without opening her eyes.

I went downstairs with the intention of asking the receptionist to call the tour guide so I could inform him of Kimberly's predicament right away. As it so happened, the guide was already downstairs talking to the receptionist about another matter. I sat down with him and apprised him of the situation. He also thought it was altitude sickness and agreed that Kimberly wasn't in any condition to travel. Oh good, I thought to myself. If he agrees with me, then perhaps he's sympathetic to our predicament and will allow us to change our travel plans without making us incur a monetary penalty. I thought wrong.

"Sorry," he said when I asked him if we could postpone our tour for one day and apply our deposit towards another day. "I already used that money to buy your bus and train ticket to Aguas Caliente for today. It's gone. I can't get it back."

That wasn't good news. "So if we don't go today, we can't get that refunded to us?" I asked to confirm.

"No," he answered quickly before proceeding to give me a lengthy explanation through somewhat broken English about how once the tickets were purchased, they're not refundable whatsoever. "You have to make up your mind right now. If you go today, we can do like we talk about. If you cancel, you lose your deposit."

Although I didn't understand every word he spoke, I did understand the conditions of the agreement. I also understood that I wasn't about to drag Kimberly all the way to Machu Pichu in her current, compromised condition.

"Do you want to go talk to your friend about it?" the guide asked me.

I recalled how Kimberly couldn't even sit upright when I was in her room minutes earlier. Not only was her illness bad, it could get worse if we forced the situation. There was no point in discussing the inevitable. "That won't be necessary," I told him. "Cancel the tour. We're staying here for today."

"That's too bad," he said.

"Yes, it is," I muttered and started to get up from the table.

Abruptly, too abruptly, the guide proposed, "Do you want to go ahead and sign up for tomorrow's tour?"

I can appreciate a guy wanting to make a buck, but this guy who'd struck me as being a little too aggressive from the start was now grating on my nerves. He knew very well that if we signed up for the next day's tour, we would have to pay him another deposit then and there. He also knew that if Kimberly was still sick the next day, we would lose our deposit yet again. "No," I replied definitively. "We're not signing up for any tour until Kimberly is feeling better."

Once I got back to my room, I called my friend and told her I'd cancelled the tour. "Get some rest," I encouraged her.

Hours later, around noon, Kimberly called my room. She sounded better and said she wanted to get out and about. We met downstairs minutes later, and I could discern she was much better. She said her headache was gone, as was her vomiting. We went on another self-guided tour of the town. Keeping with the directional caution we used the night before, we stuck close to the city square so we could always have a reference point to which we could return. As we strolled around, we took note of the many places around the Plaza de Armas square that sold tour packages to Machu Pichu. Towards the middle of the afternoon, Kimberly said she felt good enough to get on the road the next day, so we proceeded to step into various tour offices and inquired about the services they offered.

The package deals that the travel agents sold to all of us tourists were practically identical to one another: A bus would pick us up at our hotel, whisk us off to see the Sacred Valley, drop us off at the town of Ollantaytambo, allow us the afternoon to have dinner there, and then put us on a train to Aguas Caliente. A guide would greet us at the train stop in Aguas Caliente, take us to the designated hotel, and wake us up bright and early the next morning to go see Machu Pichu. Another guide, an English-speaking person, would lead us through the entire site to give us a walking history lesson of the famed ruins. Afterwards, we would return to the hotel, collect our belongings, and take a train back to Poroy where we could catch a cab to hop over to Cusco.

I wasn't surprised that all the tours were nearly identical. With numerous years of travel under my belt, I knew enough about the tourism industry to know that the actual tours were carried out by only a few companies and that the individual offices were the middlemen who funneled the tourists to those few companies.

The competing companies charged a set fee, and the individual tour offices made their money by charging a handling fee for the tours they sold. The profits that these middlemen made were the difference between what the companies charged them and what they charged the tourists. Due to the competitive factors, virtually all the offices had a threshold as to how low they could go. Subsequently, once a tourist began to bargain – as Kimberly did with great gusto – she was bound to encounter that low threshold sooner or later. More often than not, we would quickly get to the bottom price within minutes, and that price would be virtually the same price as the one we received from the previous tour office.

At the fifth travel agent we visited, we encountered Lucia, a young lady about twenty-four years old. Our conversation with her wasn't easy. Her English was very limited, and the words that were within her limits were spoken with such a thick accent that we virtually needed a sharp hacksaw to cut through them. After some spirited bargaining, we reached a rate comparable to that offered by the previous offices. I thought we'd reached the low point until Kimberly gave it one final push and asked Lucia to shave a few more dollars off her price. I was prepared to hear Lucia say the Spanish equivalent of: "Sorry, lady. At that price, I might as well board up my windows and lock my doors because I would be going out of business right away." To my surprise, she agreed to Kimberly's request, practically carving out a new bottom-of-the-barrel price!

Without any hesitation, Lucia asked us for our money. There were a few details of the tour that was still vague to me. Before handing over our cash, I asked Lucia to clarify those details. She said her English wasn't good enough to explain all the details. (This wasn't far-fetched because I barely understood her when she said her English wasn't good enough to explain all the details. She added that the English-speaking tour guide who was scheduled to meet us in the morning would be able to tell us everything we needed to know. I was slightly uneasy with this explanation but chalked it up to an unavoidable consequence of our language barrier. Foolishly, I went along with her convenient excuse. As Kimberly and I handed her our payment, I idiotically ignored the two gnawing feelings squirming around in my gut:

1) Lucia agreed to a price that was too good to be true.
2) She was in too much of a hurry to take our money and seal the deal.

The next morning arrived without a phone call from Kimberly reporting a bad headache or a bout of all-night vomiting, thank goodness. We ate breakfast and were more than ready to go by the time the bus arrived to pick us up. As the tour guide herded us onto the bus to join all the other tourists, I tried to get him to clarify what Lucia couldn't. He told me not to worry and that he would explain all of it on the way to our destination. I believed him, further tightening the dunce cap on my head.

The ride to the Sacred Valley was quite scenic. The jutting mountains and the lush, undulating landscape didn't shy away from flaunting their emerald shades of green. After visiting the village of Pisac, the bus dropped us off at the town of Ollantaytambo around dinner time. Kimberly and I thought everyone in our tour group was also stopping there. To our surprise, only eight of the thirty people in the group got dropped off. Everyone else proceeded onward to . . . somewhere else. Even more surprising was the fact that our tour guide was leaving the eight of us there to fend for ourselves. I'd been on a bunch of tours in my travels. Not once has the tour guide ever taken off and told a fragment of the group that they were now on their own. It wasn't until I inquired further that the tour guide told us we would be spending the evening at a restaurant in the center of town, and hours after that, we would have to walk about a mile down the road to get to the railroad station to catch the train that would take us to Aguas Caliente.

"What about our train tickets to get back to Cusco the next day?" I asked the tour guide.

As he quickly hopped back on the bus, he told me that I should inquire at the train station down the road and that they would tell me everything I needed to know. Miffed at the runaround I was getting but not knowing what else I could do about it, I went along with the program and hoped that the people at the train station would do as the tour guide said.

The restaurant that was our designated waiting spot was comfortable enough. It also provided us with some warmth to ward off the chill of the coming night. We ordered dinner, and as much as I would like to say the food was delicious, I can't.

I ordered a soup. I forgot what kind of soup it was, but it doesn't really matter. The appearance and taste of that watery concoction made it easily forgettable. Kimberly ordered something that turned out to be just as unpalatable. We deliberated and decided we couldn't go wrong with pizza since it was basically dough and tomato sauce. We ordered a pizza. It arrived twenty minutes later. Fortunately, we were right in that we couldn't go wrong. It was dough and tomato sauce and was neither good nor bad.

Although the night air was on the chilly side, it wasn't unpleasant. I actually welcomed the cool air in anticipation of the long walk ahead, a walk that could make us sweaty if the night was hot. At the prescribed time, Kimberly and I heaved our bags down the stairs and started hiking to the railroad station. After having sat around at the restaurant for several hours, the invigorating walk did us good. We arrived at the train station with a bright outlook for the rest of the trip.

Then we made our next discovery.

At the station, we presented our train tickets to Aguas Caliente to the lady behind the glass window. She told us where to line up for the train. We asked about our train tickets for the return trip the next day – only to hear her say she didn't know anything about that. Perplexed, I said that Lucia had told us to ask the tour guide, who in turn told us to ask her about the tickets to Cusco. Again, she said she didn't know anything about that. I showed her the receipt we received from Lucia. With a shrug, she said the receipt didn't mean anything unless we had the actual train tickets. I told her we didn't have those tickets despite repeatedly inquiring about them. She said as far as she knew, something was wrong and that we should have received our return tickets by now. As it was, she strongly recommended we buy a new set of tickets right away. If we waited until the next day, the return tickets might be sold out.

Shocked, Kimberly and I stepped back to talk it over.

Had we missed something? Was there a remote chance we had the return train tickets somewhere in our possession and didn't know it? We rifled through the few tour documents that we had. No, we didn't have the tickets. We hadn't missed anything. We had everything we were supposed to have, or to better phrase it, we had everything that Lucia deemed to give us, and nowhere in our possession were the return tickets.

What happened? Kimberly and I asked ourselves. *Had Lucia done something wrong?*

Obviously, she had, or else we would have the return tickets on our persons or in our bags. Now, it was only a question of whether Lucia's wrongdoing was an honest mistake or an intentional one.

We discussed trying to reach Lucia. The office number was on the receipt. However, it was late at night. We doubted the office was still open. Furthermore, there was the ever-present language barrier. Most pressing though was the fact that the train to Aguas Caliente was departing within minutes. If we weren't on it, we would have another issue to contend with. Time was ticking, and we needed to decide whether to buy the return tickets right away, or wait until after we had reached Lucia and risk having the tickets be sold out. We decided to err on the side of safety. We bought the return tickets right away.

Having secured our passage back to Cusco, we boarded the train to Aguas Caliente. We quickly found our seats, sat back for the hours-long ride to the base of Machu Pichu, and dozed off to the soothing, rhythmic, clickety-clack of the iron wheels beneath us.

With a few toot-toots and a couple of braking lurches, our train came to a stop in Aguas Caliente. As everyone stepped down from the cars, all of us began to notice the various porters holding up the signs of the hotels they represented. Kimberly and I saw the sign for our hotel. Along with a few other tourists, we went up to the porter to inform him we were scheduled to stay at his hotel for the night. As the other tourists told him their names, the porter – a small man in his forties and healthily fitted into a lean frame – went down the list of names on his clipboard to confirm they had a room waiting for them. Kimberly and I expected the same result when we told him our names. To our dismay, the porter told us we weren't on the list.

"I not see your names," he said.

"You don't?" I responded. "Can you look again?"

The porter looked again, moving his pencil down the list of names. He reached the bottom and shook his head. "No, I not see your names."

Kimberly and I traded looks of concern. I could tell she was thinking the same thing I was: *First, we discovered we didn't have the train tickets back to Cusco, and now our names aren't on the hotel list. Something was definitely wrong.*

I returned my attention to the porter. "What should we do?"

He thought it over for a second and said, "You come to hotel with me. Maybe someone make a mistake."

The advice was as good as any. Here it was, nearing midnight, and we were in a strange town without a clue as to where to go and what to do. Our best hope was to follow the porter to the hotel, pray that an honest mistake had been made, and hopefully find an easy fix. Besides, the sky was starting to shower slightly, and neither Kimberly nor I had brought an umbrella. Any promise for some shelter would be most welcomed.

Our trip thus far had been an uphill struggle, figuratively. Little did I know that it was about to become an uphill struggle, literally. I'd hoped that our hotel was a short walk around the corner. It wasn't. It was up a hill, around a corner . . . then up another hill, around another corner . . . then up another hill, around another corner . . .

I shouldn't have been surprised. Machu Pichu is, of course, situated on top of a mountain. It stood to reason that the surrounding towns would also be tucked into the sides of a mountain and, therefore, be comprised of angular, upward paths disguised as streets. With one hand on the handle of my rollerboard luggage and the other hand wrapped around the straps of my tote bag, I strained up one hill, turned a corner, fought my way up another hill, turned another corner, labored up another hill, and kept pushing myself to go on and on – all the while getting sprayed by the cold water that was coming down more heavily from the dark sky. Shortly after we turned the second corner, I had to stop and catch my gasping breath.

117

What else could go wrong? I wondered, huffing and puffing.

KA-BOOM!

A thunderous roar joined forces with a flash of lightning to announce a rancorous reply from the sky.

Dazed in disbelief, I looked up at the night canopy that had decided to crank up the waterworks, turning the sprinkling into a significant pour. Were there some Machu Pichu gods somewhere, I asked myself, who were testing my resolve to see the famed ruins? If there were, they were in for a disappointment. I was determined to see the walls and stones of Machu Pichu, even if it meant I had to keep climbing all night.

Finally, after turning yet another corner and scampering up yet another steep hill, we arrived at the hotel and stepped out of the unwelcoming rain. (Stooped over while still huffing and puffing, I realized why the hotel porter was so fit. Anyone trekking up and down that mountainside all day long was bound to be fit.) Kimberly and I took a seat as the other tourists checked in. We flicked the film of rainwater off of us as the other travelers got their keys and went to their rooms. When it was our turn at the counter, we asked the receptionist, a middle-age woman with an earnest air about her, to look in the computer to see if perhaps there'd been a mistake of some sort. She did as we requested and confirmed what the porter had told us – that our names were not in hotel system. I produced the receipt Lucia had written out for us. I showed the receptionist where Lucia had written down that we were supposed to get two hotel rooms. I also pointed out the price tag that we paid for our packaged tour. The receptionist nodded in comprehension. She took the receipt from me and gave it a closer inspection, then she asked me where the reference number was for our rooms.

"What reference number?" I returned with a question of my own.

She pointed to the top, right corner of the receipt. "You should have a reference number here for the rooms. There aren't any. That means you don't have any rooms reserved."

Kimberly chimed in and explained to the receptionist, "Lucia . . . the sales girl . . . she never said anything about any reference number!"

The woman behind the counter handed the receipt back to me and said matter-of-factly, "I'm sorry. Lucia . . . she did not reserve any rooms for you. Do you want me to call her?"

It was past midnight. I doubted if Lucia was still at her office. Still, it wouldn't hurt to try. "Yeah," I answered. "Can you try and call her?"

"Sure." The sympathetic woman picked up her cell phone and dialed the number on the receipt. It rang, and rang, and rang. With no reply as the expected result, she hung up.

The writing was on the wall for us. Actually, in our case, it was practically carved into the mountainside in huge, ominous letters. Lucia had pulled a fast one on us. She took our money for a whole tour but only gave us half a tour. She got us to Machu Pichu but didn't provide the means to get us back.

Then another worrisome thought struck me.

I suddenly got the gut-gnawing suspicion that since Lucia didn't supply us with the train tickets for the return trip or the hotel rooms for the night, she also didn't set up a tour of Machu Pichu the next day either.

"We also paid for a tour of Machu Pichu with a tour guide tomorrow," I conveyed to the receptionist. "I guess there's no record of that either."

The receptionist checked her records. "No," she confirmed with dejection. "No tour set up for tomorrow."

When it rains, it pours – literally and figuratively in our fiasco.

Kimberly looked at me and sighed. "What do you want to do, Nick?"

The question was perfunctory. Kimberly was a bright girl. She knew what we had to do. She knew that if we wanted to continue with our quest to see Machu Pichu, we would have to dig into our pockets again and pay what we had already paid Lucia. I took the cue in stride and queried the receptionist, "How much is it for two rooms here?"

She told me the price.

"Also," I continued to get the matter over with, "how much for Machu Pichu, for the entrance fee and tour guide?"

She told me the price.

"If we pay you now, can you set up the tour for us tomorrow?"

"Yes."

I looked over at Kimberly. "I don't see any other way around this."

"Me neither," she agreed.

The two of us must have looked pretty pathetic because the receptionist made a last ditch effort to help us out. "You don't pay me now," she said. "I will call Lucia again tomorrow morning. If she doesn't answer, then you pay me. Okay?"

That was more than fair. "Thanks," I replied.

"Yes, thanks," Kimberly added.

We received our keys and trudged off to our rooms. My room was cold. The absence of a thermostat told me there was no central heat. I looked around the room. There wasn't a portable heater in sight either. It looked like it was going to be a cold night. I didn't care. It was past midnight and we needed to get up before sunrise to begin the tour. I shed my wet clothes, put on some dry ones – bundling up along the way – and crawled into bed to squeeze in as much sleep as I could.

After Kimberly and I finished breakfast the next day, the receptionist tried once more to contact Lucia. As expected, she couldn't reach our con artist. She asked us if we wanted her to keep trying. We told her not to bother. It was a matter we would contend with once we returned to Cusco. Without further adieu, we paid her for the rooms and the tour and got on the bus to Machu Pichu.

Back and forth, in a horizontal method to accommodate for the sharp, steep climb, our bus took long, side-winding roads up the misty mountain. The drive itself gave me an immediate respect for the people who originally built the city. I was getting winded just sitting on the bus. I couldn't fathom the hellish exertion the laborers must have endured when they had to lug countless, gigantic slabs of stone for miles up the mountain. Personally, if I'd been condemned to such a hernia-inducing task, I think I would have given up after moving a single slab a single inch.

We arrived at the entrance and joined the beehive of other tourists loitering about, waiting for the international monument to open its gates. When the time arrived, we entered the grounds of the hallowed site and walked up a steep path lined with trees. Minutes later, we rounded a corner, emerged from the trees, and came upon the sight that made all the tribulations of getting to Machu Pichu worth it.

The morning sun had ascended to its throne in the sky. The mist had excused itself for the day. Before us lay the grandeur of Machu Pichu swathed in golden sunlight.

Everyone whipped out their cameras and started taking photos of the venerable gift that history had unwrapped for us. One by one, we captured the sight that we'd seen only in history books. Angle by angle, we sought to imprint the majestic vista into the definitive frames of our cameras.

And that was pretty much how it went for our entire homage.

We were constantly hopscotching from one spot to another, clicking and ooohhh-ing and aaahhh-ing at the marvelous scenery all around us. At one point, I couldn't help but compare Machu Pichu to a symbol of royalty. As is common knowledge, a crown is a cylindrical object ringed by spires of jewels. Machu Pichu is really no different. It's essentially a nature-made crown ringed by mountain tops serving as spires glittering like jewels in the morning sunlight.

Shortly after high noon, Kimberly and I began to make our way back to the entrance gate, petting one of the many llamas that grazed languidly among the tourists along the way. Although we hadn't quite satisfied our thirst for the historical site, we knew we needed to get back to Aguas Caliente in order to begin our long train ride back to Cusco. Our bus coasted down the winding road and deposited us near the town center.

We ate lunch, retrieved our bags from the hotel, and found our way to the train station.

When Kimberly and I took the train the night before from Ollantaytambo to Aguas Caliente, we didn't receive any kind of refreshments. We assumed we would be getting the same Spartan treatment on our way to Cusco. Unbeknownst to us, the train we were taking back was the Vistadome which was a step up from the Backpacker Express that got us to Aguas Caliente. Essentially, we'd inadvertently upgraded from Coach to Business Class. As a result, we were pampered with some fine wining and dining.

The meal was tasty. Although I can't recall exactly what the entrée was, I do remember that it was about on par with the First Class meal we enjoyed on the flight from Houston to Lima. After the fine dining was done, we prepared to sit back and relax when, to our surprise, the evening show began.

Yes. That's right. A show.

Out of the passengers' view, the very same train attendants who had served us our dinner got out of their uniforms and hopped into some fancy threads to put on a modeling show for us.

An announcement came over the P.A. to inform us passengers that the attendants had a variety of clothes they'd like to offer for sale. He said the clothes couldn't go wrong on us, and to demonstrate, he'd gotten the train attendants to parade down the aisle wearing an array of wardrobes.

The next thing we knew, the sound of upbeat, thrumming music began to pulsate from the speakers all around us! The door at the front of the car flew open! And our newly-attired train attendants shot out into the cabin, dancing to the beat of lively music!

As all of us passengers let out a cheer, one attendant in her early twenties paraded down the aisle as though she was sashaying down the catwalk of a Parisian fashion show, brandishing a smile that gleamed with glee. When she reached the end of the car, she swiveled and strutted back to front where she gave a short pause, bowed, and made a festive exit out the door.

No sooner than she'd stepped out of sight, the door flew open again, and out came a young man who flashed a smile at us and began to clap his hands in rhythm to nudge us audience members to put our hands together and give him a synchronized accompaniment. We eagerly complied, and he succinctly shuffled down the aisle wearing a sweater made of fine llama wool that I would never see in my shopping spree at Wal-Mart.

A few minutes after that, another attendant sprang out sporting a new outfit for us passengers to behold. After she exited the car, another attendant enthusiastically emerged to take her place, then another . . . and another . . . and another . . . until all of us spectators were giddy with fervor.

About half an hour later, as all the attendants were taking a final bow and accepting the appreciative applause heaped upon them, I couldn't help but make a comparison between the duties required of these train attendants and that required of Kimberly and me as flight attendants. As the staff on an airplane, I couldn't imagine myself providing a meal service, then put away my cart and quickly don some fancy attire and go parading around in front of a hundred cheering and clapping passengers. If that scenario were to ever come true, I would pity not only myself but also the passengers who had to witness my misguided fashion show. I think if I were to ever strut down the aisle to the beat of pulsating music, I'm 99.99% certain the passengers would immediately call to mind the advice that we flight attendants give them during the pre-flight safety demonstration: *Keep in mind that your nearest exits may be behind you!*

Darkness had set in by the time we disembarked at Poroy. Kimberly negotiated a taxi for our ride to Cusco. On the short drive there, she and I discussed how we wanted to approach Lucia and get our money back. We kept in mind that early the next morning we would have to fly from Cusco to Lima which meant we had to resolve the matter that night. From what we could gather, the tourist offices closed around 9 p.m.

Consequently, we had to hurry to get the job done. The two of us were also fairly certain we had to get the police involved. The part that was nebulous was whether we should confront Lucia first, then go get the police if she refused to give us a refund. Or should get the police first, then confront Lucia with the authorities at our side to prevent her from even thinking about refusing our refund?

We decided on the latter. If we went with the former and showed up without any law enforcement in tow, Lucia could easily deny any wrongdoing and force us to go get the police. As soon as we left, she could quickly slip out the door and be long gone by the time we returned with the police. Given that she had cheated us already, we had no doubt she would cheat us again to avoid being held accountable for her original dishonest deed.

One element that helped us decide we should get the police before we went to Lucia's office was the fact that there was a small police station just a few doors down from Lucia's office.

We reached our hotel, tossed our bags into our rooms without unpacking them, and hurried towards the town square. Minutes later, we were inside the police station, ready and eager to tell them what Lucia had done. Unfortunately, a few aggravating factors tripped us up right away. The first was that no one at the police station spoke English. One of the policemen had to lead us next door to a hotel where the English-speaking receptionist could translate our account to him. Once the policeman heard our account in Spanish, he us his reply, and we were dismayed to hear that we were at the wrong police station.

"Wrong police station?" I asked the cop with the help of the receptionist. Yes, the officer relayed to us, before adding on that the type of police station we wanted was the tourist police, not the regular police. He told us we had to go elsewhere to get the tourist police.

Kimberly looked at me with puzzlement, and I could see my questions reflected in her eyes: *Why are there two types of police stations? More to the point, we were standing in the middle of the tourist area. If there was any place for the tourist police, this would be it.*

The policeman read our expressions, understood, and shook his head with a smile. He said something to the receptionist, and the two of them led Kimberly and me outside to a taxi. The receptionist spoke to the driver. The driver nodded. The receptionist motioned for us to get in the back seat.

I turned to Kimberly and mumbled, "I guess we're taking a taxi to the tourist police. Maybe we should go and confront Lucia first."

"No," Kimberly countered. "We need the police before we go see Lucia."

My skepticism was growing. Maybe getting the police first wasn't the best option. Nevertheless, I went along with Kimberly's preference. I asked the driver how much the cab fare would be: "Cuantos?"

He told me the amount. It wasn't much. I equated the low fare to a short drive and hypothesized we would be able to quickly get there and back before Lucia closed her office for the night.

Kimberly and I got in. The driver drove us out of the main square into another part of the city . . . and he drove . . . and he drove . . . and he drove. The driver kept driving for much longer than I expected. It was one of the few taxi rides in my life where I wished I was getting less than what I paid for. Eventually, we arrived at another police station.

The driver came to a stop and called out to a uniformed officer standing on the front steps. The policeman walked over to us. The driver said something to him. The officer turned to Kimberly and me. "Tourist police?" he asked.

"Yes," I confirmed.

He pointed down the street and said, "Different building."

We're still not at the tourist police station? I was dumbfounded. Before I could verbalize this incredulity to the new policeman, our driver put the car in gear and took off again.

I shook my head at the time we were wasting, dejected that our chances of getting a refund was slipping away by the minute.

Lady luck intervened and gave my spirit a lift. Half a block down the street, our driver abruptly pulled over and pointed us to a two-story building. "Police," he said.

Finally, we had arrived at the tourist police station. We paid him, got out, and walked to the small building. I sized up the place, and if I had to make a guess, I'd say that this part of the police station was an overflow building of some sort, and that the main station got too crowded, so the powers that be put the tourist services in this little outcropping. At any rate, when Kimberly and I went inside, we were directed upstairs. Once we got up there, we were told to wait outside a small office. We took a seat and waited, and waited, and waited.

While we waited, we struck up a conversation with a couple who had also come to report a crime. She was Peruvian. He was European. They'd had their money stolen in a robbery. Judging by their downcast disposition, it was safe to say they lost more than Kimberly and I did.

The office wasn't exactly a beehive of activity, but since there were only two or three officers on duty to interview all the people coming in to report their crimes, the process was painstakingly slow. Ten minutes after Kimberly and I had sat down, the police still hadn't tended to the couple who was there before us, which meant it would take them that much longer to tend to my friend and me.

The minutes callously crept by as though they were comprised of 120 seconds instead of 60. Eventually, the couple before us was called in. Kimberly and I waited some more, subjecting ourselves to the mercy of the seconds that crawled by like soldiers cautiously trying to cross a treacherous mine field.

I couldn't take it anymore. I jumped up and told Kimberly, "This was a mistake! We shouldn't have come here. It's taking forever. If we leave now, maybe we can still catch Lucia at her office!" I shot for the stairs.

"Wait!" Kimberly urged me.

Very reluctantly, I gave pause.

Kimberly got up, but instead of coming towards the stairs where I was, she walked right into the policemen's office and calmly said to them, "Excuse me. We really need to see someone right now."

To my complete surprise, one of the policemen simply replied, "Okay. Come in."

Just like that, Kimberly's calm, composed demeanor got us in the door.

We sat down. The officer, a clean cut guy in his twenties, took down our report. He asked us how we wanted to resolve the matter. We told him we needed a policeman to come with us to Lucia's office to persuade the licentious crook to give us our money back. He said he could accommodate us, but we would have to wait downstairs for the next available unit. Having no other choice, Kimberly and I went downstairs and waited some more.

The seconds that had earlier crawled by like soldiers crossing a mine field must have detonated a few of the mines because they seemed to have come to a stop altogether. After glancing at my watch countless times, I began to resign myself to the fact that Lucia's office would be closed by the time we got there and that we would have to fly back to Lima early the next morning without our refund. Oh, well, I comforted myself. At least we accomplished what we wanted to. At least we succeeded in visiting Machu Pichu.

I'm not sure how much time we lost while waiting there. Fifteen minutes? Half an hour? Almost an hour? All I recall is that when a police car finally pulled up and the two policemen told Kimberly and me to get in, we quickly got in.

The older officer was in his late forties. For some reason, he struck me as a "Pedro." The younger officer behind the wheel couldn't have been more than twenty-five. He struck me as a "Francisco." Thankfully, Pedro spoke a smattering of English, allowing us to relate the ordeal to him. He nodded in comprehension at the end of our explanation and relayed the gist of our account to his partner in Spanish.

Whether it was because my explanation in the car was too long-winded or because Francisco took a few short cuts, before I realized it, we were pulling up in front of Lucia's office. The moment the car came to a stop, Kimberly threw open the door and leaped out of the car, looking a lot like the actress Lucy Liu in the movie "Charlie's Angels." The officers and I hurried to catch up with our newly-minted crime fighter, rushing through the front door in the wake of Kimberly's exuberant entrance. Once inside, we saw that our intention of catching Lucia by surprise had most of its desired effect. The handful of office workers who were still present reacted with shock at our abrupt appearance. The one person whom we truly wanted to catch off-guard, however, was nowhere in sight.

Lucifer . . . I mean Lucia . . . was absent and unaccounted for. Kimberly asked her colleagues where she was. They said she'd taken the day off. They asked us what we wanted with her. Pedro conveyed our account to them. One young lady in the group said she was a personal friend of Lucia's and didn't think Lucia would ever do such a thing. I pulled out the pertinent paperwork and showed all of it to the colleague, a person whom I'll refer to as "Angela" for the angelic act she would do for us. The first piece of evidence I showed Angela was the receipt. Like the receptionist at the hotel in Aguas Caliente, Angela noted the missing reference number for the hotel rooms and the Machu Pichu tour. Next, I directed Angela's attention to the train tickets we had to buy ourselves to return to Cusco, tickets that should have been paid for already.

Angela's expression grew from concerned to greatly troubled. Although she didn't want to believe that Lucia had stolen $260 from Kimberly and me, the evidence of her friend's egregious act was staring at her in the face. Angela said she had Lucia's personal phone number and would call her. She took out her cell phone and dialed the number. The phone on the other end rang and rang and rang. After about fifteen rings, Angela got the same result as the hotel receptionist in Aguas Caliente. She hung up then promptly apologized to Kimberly and me on behalf of Lucia. She added that she would tell Lucia to give us a refund the first thing in the morning. Kimberly told her that wasn't feasible because we were checking out of our hotel before sunrise to get to the airport.

Angela said she didn't know what more she could do. She sounded earnest enough, and I wasn't sure what more she could do either. At a loss for options, I was somewhat prepared to accept our monetary loss when Pedro intervened on our behalf and began speaking directly to Angela. The two of them engaged in a short conversation that ended with Angela turning to Kimberly and me and saying, "I have two hundred dollars in my desk. That's all I have. I give you two hundred. Lucia pay me back when I see her. Okay?"

I glanced at Kimberly. She glanced at me. The consensus was as clear as it was concise: *This was as good as it was going to get. We'd be wise to accept it and move on.*

Kimberly gave Angela a consenting nod. "Yes. Okay."

As Angela went to her desk to retrieve the cash, the two officers worked with another member of the staff to produce a pen, a sheet of paper – and oddly enough – an ink pad. I gathered that they wanted the pen and paper to put the agreement in writing. I didn't know what the ink pad was for though. As I mused over this over, Angela came back to Kimberly and me. Hesitantly, she said, "Sorry, I only have $120. Can I give you $120, not $200?"

Great, I laughed ruefully in my mind. As soon as we agreed to $200, she switched it to $120. "I can't believe this," I said in disbelief.

The supervising officer, unaware of Angela's revision, came over to us and started to show us the sheet of paper on which he'd just written an explanation and a statement. "This is the agreement. You sign here," he instructed me.

"I'm not so sure if we can," I told Pedro.

"Why?" he asked me quizzically.

I flicked a thumb over at Angela and said, "She just told me she doesn't have the $200. She only has $120."

Pedro pivoted towards Angela. He raised an eyebrow, silently and unmistakably asking her if what I said was true.

Angela answered with a sheepish smile, silently and unmistakably confirming that my words were correct.

In the snap of a finger, Pedro launched into a sharp rebuke, lambasting Angela for what Lucia had done and for the way she herself was handling the situation. Linguistically, I had no idea what the man was saying. Realistically, I understood everything he was declaring. The reproach amounted to:

> "Angela, are you trying to play games with me? First, Lucia cheats these two tourists out of their money. She leaves them stranded in Aguas Caliente without a hotel, a tour of Machu Pichu, and a train ride back to Cusco. They come to me asking for help. You offer them $200 and ask them to settle for that amount instead of the $260 that Lucia stole from them. They agree to it, and as soon as they agree to it, you change the amount to $120? You can't do that! We already agreed to the $200. Plus, I just wrote out an agreement saying you're refunding them $200. If they agree to $120, what are you going to do next? Change the amount to $80. I won't let you do that. You agreed to $200. You have to stick to that amount!"

The tongue-lashing did its job. Angela quickly became remorseful. She mumbled something to Pedro then told Kimberly and me, "Okay. I only have $120 in U.S. dollars. I can give you the rest in Peruvian soles. That's $80 in Peruvian money. Is that okay?"

I didn't need to check with Kimberly to know the necessary answer. It was plainly clear that the longer we remained stuck in this quagmire, the worse it would get. If part of our payment was going to be in Peruvian soles instead of U.S. dollars, we were only too happy to take our money and run.

"That's fine," I told Angela. "We can accept the money in dollars and soles."

"Thank you," she replied and returned to her desk to get the money.

Looking satisfied that his stern lecture had done its job, Pedro handed Kimberly a clipboard and pen. He pointed to the piece of paper on the clipboard and said, "Write your name and your nationality, please."

"Sure," Kimberly said and began to write her name and nationality. When she was finished, Pedro pointed to her last name, a surname that happens to contain the letter "H."

"H," Pedro commented.

Like me, Kimberly thought he was stating there was an "H" in her last name. Like me, Kimberly interpreted his comment to be somewhat odd and irrelevant. Even so, she addressed it as I would have. She politely confirmed that the letter was as he observed. "Yes, that's an H."

Pedro shook his head. "No," he said, pointing to her surname again as he repeated, "H."

My travel companion gave me a puzzled look. She was evidently wondering why Pedro was fixated on the letter "H" in her last name. Was he having trouble reading her handwriting? Was he trying to clarify that there was an "H" in her surname? If he was, she just confirmed that there was. Why was he still asking if it there was an "H" in her name. Not knowing what more she could do, Kimberly did the only thing she could. Again, she told Pedro, "Yes, that's an H."

Pedro shook his head again in slight frustration to relay to Kimberly and me that we weren't getting the message. Once more, he pointed at Kimberly's last name and said, "No, I mean H!"

My friend and I were mystified. Why was Pedro persistently asking if there was an "H" in her last name?

Suddenly, the comprehension hit both of us at once. When we checked in at the hotel in Cusco and Aguas Caliente, the receptionist in both places asked us to write down our name, nationality, and *age*. As far as the name and nationality parts were concerned, we could understand why they might want that information, but as far as our age was concerned, we had no clue as to why they wanted that tidbit. Nevertheless, we went ahead and did as they asked. So with all that in mind, it finally dawned on Kimberly and me that Pedro was telling Kimberly to write down her **age** next to her last name.

"Oh," Kimberly laughed with delight. "You want my age!"

"Yes, that's what I said," Pedro declared as if the matter should have been obvious all along. "Write your H!"

And while Kimberly commenced to put down how old she was next to her name, I had to marvel upon the similarity between the letter "H" and the pronunciation of the word "age." I had never realized how much alike they sounded, and I could easily see how a non-native English speaker would have trouble distinguishing the hue of difference between the letter "H" and the word "age."

After Kimberly was done, I jotted down my name, nationality, and "H." Pedro then motioned for me to come over to the desk where he had placed the written agreement next to an ink pad. "Your fingers, please," he told me.

So that's what the ink pad was for! Apparently, in Peru, they didn't go by your John Hancock. They went by your fingerprints instead. In a way, I could understand that rationale since signatures could be forged but fingerprints couldn't.

"You want me to put down my fingerprints?" I asked Pedro.

"Yes," he replied matter-of-factly.

I took a look at the document. It was all in Spanish. For all I knew, it could have been saying that I agreed to give up my first-born child. "Um, uh," I stammered to the police officer, "I don't mind my giving you my fingerprints, but this is all in Spanish. I don't know what it's saying."

The veteran police officer took in a deep breath. It wasn't hard to discern that he was trying to calm himself. He pointed to the document and stated, "It say what we talk about."

"But," I stammered, "I don't know Spanish. I don't know what it says."

He took a deeper breath. I could see him wanting to unleash the same lecture on me that he unleashed on Angela moments ago. If he had, I'm quite certain his lecture would have declared:

Look here, you nitwit. If you think about it, you can see that there's no way around this. It's unfortunate that Lucia took a good chunk of your money and ran away with it. It is fortunate, however, that her friend, Angela, was kind enough to step up to the plate and give you back most of your money. Like she told you, she will bring this matter to Lucia's attention tomorrow morning. When she does, two things can happen. Lucia can 'fess up and admit everything that she did and reimburse Angela for the $200 she's paying you. Or, she can continue with the con job and profess she doesn't know anything about this incident. If she goes with the con job, Angela has to have a way to prove that she gave you $200. She has to have something in writing to show the authorities. That's what this written document and your fingerprints are for. Got it? Now if you'll cooperate with me, we'll get this done, and you will get your $200 refund. If not, you're walking out of here empty-handed.

Since I didn't want to be lashed with such a lecture and since I did want to get our refund, I said to Pedro, "Okay, I can give you my fingerprints," and promptly provided my full cooperation. Pedro commenced to take my fingerprints and did the same with Kimberly. Once we were done, Angela brought out the money and counted out what she promised: $120 in dollars and $80 in soles.

Kimberly and I had gotten most of our money back. We were able to get that partial refund because the police were there to reinforce our position. The police were there to help us because Kimberly was calm-minded enough to tell me to stop in my tracks when I was ready to bolt from the police station and rush over to Lucia's office before it closed. The police were present to resolve the matter suitably because Kimberly was neutral-minded enough to simply waltz into the busy policemen's office and tell them we needed to talk to someone right away. In short, we had most of our refund in hand because we did it Kimberly's way, not mine.

My friend and I had sealed the deal. With our task completed, Kimberly and I thanked Angela for her help. Pedro and Francisco offered us a ride back to our hotel. We accepted, and they chauffeured us up the road to our accommodations for the night.

The next morning, my companion and I greeted the waking sun as we arrived at the airport. We checked in, boarded the plane, and took off for Lima – this time without any airline staff telling me I had to get off the plane because they couldn't find my ticket.

Ingrid, our friend who lives in Lima, met us at the airport. She took us to her home and made us feel at home for the weekend. For the next couple of days, she showed us the highlights of Lima and feted us with her mom's fine cooking.

Sunday night arrived too soon. Kimberly and I didn't want to wear out our welcome, so we bid Ingrid and her parents a muchos gracias for their hospitality before taking a taxi to the airport. Sated with the adventures of our trip, my traveling companion and I flew home, gladdened that we had gone onward and upward to Machu Pichu!

For The Sake Of Society

Maintaining a neutral mindset and reaping its rewards is good for more than just the individual. It's also good for the sake of society. A few instances come to mind, one of which involved me not being as neutral as I should have been.

~

The moment actually ran tangent to being a fence sitter and me doing something when I should have been doing nothing.

The year was around 2001. The internet was firing up its rockets to launch into the stratosphere. I received an email from a friend of mine saying that computers everywhere were infected with a harmful virus, and that I had to click on the link in the email to download a program that would get rid of the virus. As soon as I read this urgent-sounding email, I automatically believed it was true and clicked on the link and downloaded the program. Unfortunately, I didn't stop there. Like my friend who had hurriedly forwarded the email to me, I also hurriedly forwarded the email to my friends and relatives to alert them about the virus.

The next day, a cousin of mine who was studying to be a computer programmer told me the email was a hoax and that whoever started the email was preying on people's fears. The link in the email that was supposedly helpful was actually harmful. In truth, clicking on it and downloading it made a person's computer more vulnerable to attacks. The schemers who started the whole ploy were using trickery to achieve illicit gains. They were employing converse psychology, deceiving people into thinking they were doing something good when they were actually doing something bad. In a way, the perpetrators were counting on people to react with emotion rather than with reason, to behave haphazardly rather than intellectually.

As I already noted, their trick easily worked on me.

Fortunately, Microsoft promptly became aware of the pervasive email and instituted an easy fix through one of their regular updates.

I greeted the news of the easy fix with much relief, especially when I learned that a couple of my friends had also automatically believed the edict in the email and had also clicked on the link to download the program. Fortunately, those friends had not forwarded my misguided warning to their friends. If they had, they could have inadvertently perpetuated a computer virus that could have exponentially multiplied and quickly wormed its way through an unsuspecting society – which, of course, was exactly what the perpetrators wanted.

After this incident, I became much more careful when acting on a "warning" that came in an email. Before I did anything, I stopped and did nothing. Then I looked into the matter before continuing, which mostly comprised of me asking my computer-programming cousin what he thought I should do.

By stopping and doing nothing, I was able to pause and accurately evaluate the situation. By taking a moment to be neutral in my reaction, I was able to *not* spread another virus.

~

As much as I cherish individual freedom, I recognize that sometimes individual freedom has to take a backseat to the needs of society.

Case in point: *Driving.*

What side of the road of do you drive on? If you live in the USA, you would naturally answer the right side. (I hope.) Have you ever stopped and wondered why you can't drive on the left side? That may seem like an odd question, but when you think about it, why shouldn't you be able to drive on the left side of the road if you feel like it? Why is it that other people have the right to demand that you drive on the right side of the road? Why can't you assert your personal freedom and drive on whatever side you want to?

You already know the answer to all that.

You don't drive on the left side of the road because everyone must agree to drive on a particular side of the road. You're a reasonable person, and because you're a reasonable person, you're willing to enter a neutral compromise for the sake of society. Just as you don't drive on the left side of the road, you also don't drive diagonally across the road, or swerve back and forth across both sides whenever you feel like it. As a result of your agreement to stay on one specific side of the road, you contribute to a society that can move in a sensible, safe manner.

And just as it's good that you agree to a neutral behavior for the benefit of society, it's also good that others do the same. Picture yourself on a country highway and driving on the right side of the road like you're supposed to, and picture the driver of the car coming towards you driving on the left side of the road (from his perspective) because he feels like it. In no time at all, you're in a head-on collision with him, all because he didn't want to submit to a neutral agreement, all because he refused to stay on the right side of the road.   Fortunately, the vast majority of us recognize the need for this neutrality. Our reward is that we can get on the road without constantly worrying about getting in a head-on collision.

Of course, the rules of society change as you change societies. If you travel abroad and find yourself zooming down the road in a country like England, or Japan, or Australia, or Thailand, you'd be wise to know that they drive on the left side of the road and that you should definitely adhere to the left side too. No matter what country you're in, it's a good bet to say that the people of that country are willing to engage in a neutral conduct so that their society can operate safely, sensibly.

~

137

As I'm cranking up my laptop to work on this book, I'm settling down from the big Christmas dinner I had at my aunt's house. A lot of my relatives live within a 20 mile radius. It's not hard for us to get together as a family. Regrettably, it is hard for some family members to get together. That's why some of the relatives who live only 10 minutes away weren't in attendance.

Something tells me you already know what I'm talking about because you're part of a family too. And since you're part of a family too, you also know all about the squabbles that can erupt like volcanoes. Most likely, you've told yourself that these frictions are inevitable because family promotes familiarity and, unfortunately, familiarity breeds contempt. Even so, I'll bet you know that contempt doesn't have to run amok. You know that it can be controlled, and a good way to do keep it controlled is to have everybody do one thing: *Keep their mouths shut.*

You're not asking for a lifelong vow of silence, right? You're a reasonable person who knows that your vast family consists of too many different personalities to ask for any extended length of zipping-up-the-mouth. You're just asking that everyone keep their polarizing opinions to themselves for a few hours so the blood relations can enjoy an evening together. You're asking for this simple acquiescence so you can chat with your aunts and uncles about their jobs, so you can catch up with the cousins whom you haven't seen in almost a year, so you can chase around the little nieces and nephews who were just learning how to walk the last time you saw them.

Are you going to get your wish?

I have my doubts.

Like me, you'll just have to make do with what you've got. All the while, you can daydream about how wonderful it would be if a few rotten apples in your family tree would take a neutral road and not say anything negative for a few short hours. (There's definitely something to be said for the fact that some things are better left unsaid.)

Since you're already dreaming, you might as well dream big. You can take note that a whole is made of its many parts and that a whole is only as good as its separate parts. From that platform, you spring upward and outward and strive to grasp the fact that it's a myriad of family trees that make up the forest of our society. You can ponder how peaceably a society would exist if all the trees in the forest would learn to be neutral while they're gathered under a singular sky, one that envelopes our only Earth.

Will your dream ever come true? Well, let's just say that you have a better chance of winning the grand prize of a multi-state lottery. That said, somebody has to win the lottery, right? And the person who won that grand prize had to buy a ticket to give herself a winning chance. So perhaps you should go ahead and daydream, and you can let that daydream be your ticket. Perhaps your daydream will encourage others to dream as well and somehow, some way, the en-masse effort will persuade all the tumultuous family trees on our singular Earth to live together agreeably, neutrally, in one big forest.

And society will be all the better for it.

~

Just as we can rationally agree that giving up something (the right to drive on any side of the road we want to, for instance) can be of benefit to ourselves (avoiding a head-on collision, for instance), it's also rational to note that accepting a loss can be of benefit to ourselves. Have you turned on the TV recently to see a chaotic scene in a foreign country where one faction has lost a presidential election and their reaction is to riot in the streets and raise havoc because they didn't get their way? You probably have because there are so many countries where society is so unstable that a political loss will turn the country into a raging war zone.

It's highly doubtful you'll see that in the USA because we, as a society, can accept a political loss without pitching the country into total anarchy. The most we will do is revel in the punchlines on late night talk shows at the expense of the candidates, poke fun at an election debacle (think "hanging chads" from the Gore vs. Bush election in the year 2000), or maybe bear witness to extensive litigation – at the worst. But that will be the extent of it.

This is partly because that's just the nature of our nation. If our candidate has lost a presidential election, we recognize that we've done all we can in this go-around and that the next best thing to do is wait 4 years and give it our all again in the next go-around. It's also partly because we innately know that it's better to accept a loss and maintain a calm state than to allow our society to disintegrate into a condition where chaos reigns supreme. Intrinsically, we know that we'll do what we need to do for the sake of our society.

~

I was working with a flight attendant not too long ago when she said something that hit me as troubling. "Janet" said she was tired of mean passengers and wasn't going to take it anymore. She also said her husband (who's not a flight attendant, in case it matters) was also tired of mean people and also wasn't going to take it anymore. As "Bob" put it, from now on, he was "No more Mr. Nice Guy." Their cumulative resolution to dealing with mean people was to be mean to others before others could be mean to them. In other words, they were going to take preemptive measures to be "pre-mean" to people.

As far as my colleague's experience with mean people was concerned, I could definitely relate. Not too long ago, I was working in the First Class section when a man in Coach with beefy shoulders and a big gut ("Bubba" I'll call him) barreled past me, plopped himself down in a First Class seat, and started talking to the guy next to him. When I saw this, I wondered: *Did this guy just upgrade himself to First Class?*

To make sure there wasn't a misunderstanding of some sort, I asked Bubba if he had a Coach ticket or First Class ticket. He said he had a Coach ticket. "In that case," I informed him, "you should return to your Coach seat." Bubba said he didn't want to. I held out hopes that he had a rational explanation and asked him why he didn't want to. With abundant audacity, he said the seat next to his buddy was empty, so he took it.

I could hardly believe my ears. Mind you, this wasn't a case of someone coming up to First Class to have a quick word with his companion. I'd had plenty of those instances and didn't mind if someone chatted for a few minutes then returned to their assigned seat. This was the case of a man wielding his intimidation to get his way. Furthermore, given the well-rehearsed way he was going about it, I'd say he'd done this many times before and gotten his way many times before. In short, this Bubba guy was a habitually mean person and profited from being a habitually mean person. That didn't sit well with me.

I asked him to return to his seat again. He refused again, literally snarling at me. Bearing in mind that I was in uniform and, therefore, had to uphold a professional conduct, I asked Bubba several more times to return to his seat. He refused several more times, each time criticizing me and claiming I was exercising poor customer service skills because I wouldn't allow him to sit in First Class for free. Finally, I told him if he didn't return to his seat in Coach, I would call the captain and we would do whatever was necessary to correct the situation. With another snarl, Bubba moved back to his original seat.

He behaved himself for the rest of the flight, but once we reached our destination, he stopped to criticize my customer service skills some more then took down my name in order to write a complaint letter to the company about me.

As you might guess, this altercation didn't exactly brighten my day. At the same time though, it didn't deaden it either. It didn't put me in such a foul mood that I wanted to take out my anger on another person. After years on the job, if there was anything I'd learned, it was how to not let a negative experience with one passenger work its way over to another passenger. I can't say I've always been successful in upholding this little ideal of mine, but at least I was aware of it and knew to reach for it.

It wouldn't be fair if I got mad at a passenger, I've told myself, just because the previous passenger did something bad to me. If I gave in to that, then I would let the anger that Bubba had inflicted upon me spill over to a passenger like Bob whose only fault was being a nice guy.

As a consequence, Bob would react negatively because all he did was be a nice guy and the reward he got for it was undeserving, bad treatment from me.

That bad treatment would be yet another negative experience in Bob's daily life, another repetition of someone being mean to him, and the compounding repetition would understandably push Bob over the edge and make him succumb to the corrosive declaration of: "No More Mr. Nice Guy!"

It's no wonder that Bob would then want to go out into the world and be mean to everybody else.

And when the people that he was mean to then made their own resolution to be mean to everyone else they encountered, they would subsequently spread the germ of meanness anywhere and everywhere.

And when those people then made their resolution to be mean to other people, they would subsequently spread the germ of meanness to everyone they came across.

And when those people then made their resolution to be mean to other people, they would spread the germ of meanness to . . .

The next thing you know, the germ of meanness has taken on the characteristics of an unstoppable virus. It has metastasized and is spreading with maniacal speed from one person to a few persons, to a small group of persons, to a bigger group of people, to an ever bigger group of people, to a . . .

While I was working on the second draft of this book, "The Walking Dead" was getting ready to start its 5th season. It's a hugely popular TV show about zombies, and just in case you're not up to speed on how the zombie world works, it goes something like this:

-    One zombie bites a person, and that person turns into a zombie.

- Those two zombies bite two more people (one person per zombie, as proper zombie etiquette dictates), and those two people turn into zombies.
- Those four zombies bite four more people (yes, still one person per zombie), and those four people turn into zombies.
- Those eight zombies bite eight more people, and . . .

Before you knew it, the whole world is overrun with zombies! (Which, in TV land, is a good thing. Otherwise, there wouldn't be such a riveting show that can me on the edge of my seat and make me a die-hard "Dead" fan.)

It doesn't take that much insight to see the parallel between the scenario of one person being mean to another person, who is then mean to another person, who is then mean to another person – and – the scenario of one zombie biting another person to create a zombie, who then bites another person to create another zombie, who then bites another person to create another zombie, who then bites . . .

In other words, contagion is exponentially contagious.

And in today's hurry-up, hyperspeed, Ultra Wi-Fi, give-it-to-me-now, instant gratification world, it's much too easy to get too angry, too fast, and too . . . out of hand.

The way I see it, there are two kinds of people in this world. There are the fair-minded people who want to play by the rules, and there are the people who want to trample on the fair-minded people who want to play by the rules. The trick for the fair-minded people is to correct the people trampling on them without harming the other fair-minded people.

Personally, I wouldn't want to bite someone and turn them into a zombie just because someone else bit me and turned me into a zombie. I'd like to think I'm better than that. I'd like to think I would take the high road when it came to all that zombie zaniness. I suppose I wouldn't know unless I'm thrown into the zombie world somehow and forced to prove my zombie mettle. If it ever came to that, however, I'm fairly confident I would make sure the zombie buck stops with me. If some knucklehead zombie ever bit me, I would certainly do my utmost to settle the matter directly with him – and only him. I would bite him back, then and there, to settle the matter with him – and only him. I wouldn't want to spread the zombie virus by biting another person who was an innocent, non-zombie bystander.

In that same vein of thought . . . and artery of aspiration, I certainly wouldn't want to perpetuate any one-directional anger syndrome in the real world that we live in. If I'm going to get mad at somebody, I'd be manly about it. (Remember, you don't have to be a real man to be manly.) I would get mad at someone deserving of it, someone who was originally mean to me – like the brute who thought he had the right to take a First Class seat just because he felt like it. I wouldn't go after someone who had nothing to do with the matter, someone who prided himself on being a nice guy, like Bob. If nothing else, I would hate to have it on my conscience that I committed an injustice upon an innocent bystander. It would make me sick to spread that sickness.

What's that, you say?

Did I just hear you ask what's a good way to stop the virus of being mean?

It's funny you should ask because I think I have a workable answer.

Before we succumb to the demands of our modern day, hurry-up world and make snap judgments that can result in the wrong decision, how about if we just take a moment to be neutral? How about if we took the bad situation we just experienced and left it inside its own casing? How about if we said the past is the past, and recognize that we're in the present? Therefore, we'll regard the current encounter that we're in as a separate identity unbound by the pesky past.

With our boundaries properly set, we can approach the new exchange and evaluate it on its own merits. We'll recognize that it might be good, or that it might be bad. Either way, we'll enter the situation with a neutral frame of mind, free of pre-judgment, free of being pre-mad.

I should point out that I have a self-interest in this approach. The way I see it, it's good for myself as well as others. In the spirit of self-preservation, I wouldn't want to be on the receiving end of anyone's mistreatment. I wouldn't want to step on a plane as a passenger and have Janet, the flight attendant, be mad at me because someone else was just mad at her.

When you think about it, we're all customers somewhere. If you come to where I work, I'm the staff and you're the customer. If I come to where you work, you're the staff and I'm the customer. As the customer on a plane, I would want to be treated right. I would want a flight attendant to perceive me as neither good nor bad. I would want that person to start her interaction with me on a clean slate and perceive me in a neutral light.

Ultimately, that's what I found troubling about Janet's comment. She and Bob were too willing to perpetuate the meanness, which stood the risk of perpetuating more meanness, which stood the risk of perpetuating more meanness, which stood the risk of . . .

Amplified to the aspects of everyday life, where would we be as a society if everyone was predisposed to being mean to everybody else because somebody was mean to them? It would be the ultimate, vicious cycle with no end in sight. It would be insanity feeding on itself and achieving gluttonous glory.

Fortunately, our society hasn't crumbled to that stage. Just as there are days of discord in my life, I'm sure there are acrimonious moments in yours. And yet, we rebound. We regain our composure. We enable ourselves to move on. Fortunately, the vast majority of us can nudge our frame of mind back to an even setting after an altercation. For the sake of society, we know how to hit the reset button and begin anew again.

~

In my line of work, I'm very appreciative that 99% of the people stepping on a plane recognize the fact that they're entering a communal space and that they have to maintain a neutral disposition to accomplish their objective: *Getting from point A to point B.*

People wanting to get from Los Angeles to New York City know that they can drive there or fly there. They know that if they drive, or take Amtrak or Greyhound, they'll have to spend about five days on the road, not to mention the cost of hotels, food, etc. They know that if they fly, they can be there in five hours. Subsequently, they agree to enclose themselves in a metallic tube with over a hundred strangers and sit quietly and uncomfortably in order to get to their destination as quickly and safely as possible. (It's undeniable that the safety numbers are better for flying than driving.)

These passengers fully realize that since they are in a public setting, they cannot do the things they would normally do at home – like talking really loudly, or cranking up the music on their portable player, or running wildly about. They agree to these restrictions because they know they're giving up something to get something. They know they're conceding some personal freedom to gain a very expeditious journey. Of course, they expect the same from the other passengers around them too. Collectively, the vast majority of people agree that once the airplane door is shut, they are in a society of their own and that for the next five hours, they need to enter a neutral territory so they can have a calm flight and get to their destination as serenely as possible.

By the way, notice that I said 99% of the people know to behave themselves on the plane. Who are the other 1%? Well, you've heard about them. They pop up in the news for doing things like getting drunk (yes, it happens), fighting with each other over a reclined seatback (it's happening more and more) and – prepare to gasp – defecating in the aisle (gross but true!).

It's a good thing that only about 1% of the flying public is non-neutral.

~

At the intersection of personal freedom and societal safety is a well known example of something you cannot do in a public place like a crowded movie theatre. You cannot falsely yell, "Fire!" Doing so may cause a stampede and could result in people getting hurt. Just as you are prohibited from falsely yelling, "Fire!" – so are the other people in the movie theatre. Their cry of alarm could cause you to get run over. Again, it's a reciprocating arrangement where all the people in that setting lose something to gain something. Collectively, everyone benefits from a neutral agreement.

Sadly, there are some who will purposely yell, "Fire!" in a movie theatre just to see people get hurt. Even more sadly, there are some who will commit acts of violence so heinous and so random that they leave the rest of us bewildered with grievous dismay. It wasn't that long ago that a gunman burst into a movie theatre and started shooting at everyone in sight. After that, another gunman went into a church and killed the worshippers on the site. After that, another gunman entered a college classroom and slaughtered many of his peers. Soon, I fear, another gunman will barge into (enter a public place here) and haphazardly massacre (enter the number of killed here) who perished while going about their everyday lives.

It's no secret that familiarity breeds contempt. It's somewhat lesser known that contempt breeds familiarity. These gunmen's contempt for society has caused so many repeated occurrences of senseless violence that the public is no longer so shocked to learn that yet another mass shooting has occurred. Like it or not, society has virtually been forced to accept these massacres as commonplace. Like it or not, the gunmen's contempt breeds our familiarity.

If there was one thing I could say to the people who commit these acts of violence, it would be, "Hold off on that. Push the reset button. Go back to neutral. Tomorrow is another day. Take another day to think it over." Maybe if these people accepted my plea, they would give pause for 24 hours, and those precious 24 hours would give them a chance to think about the grief they're about to inflict. During that time, their victims would gain another day on earth. During that time, these takers-of-lives might decide not to go through with their deed, or they might push the reset button yet again to delay their deed again by another day, and hopefully they'll keep resetting that button until they decide not to go through with it at all. Hopefully, they'll find their neutral mode and stay there, and society will be much better for it.

Regrettably, as I'm typing this sentence, another deadly shooting has appeared in the news. As a result, the debate about gun control has been brought to the forefront once again. The pointed question remains the same: *Should we institute gun control and make firearms illegal to private citizens, or should we leave the laws as they are and pray that another random act of violence won't happen?*

Allow me to put in my two cents worth.

Neither option is viable.

Making all guns illegal might have a chance if it resolves the crucial question: *Will removing guns from private citizens cure society of this abhorrent ailment?*

The answer is No. The people who commit these crimes are mentally ill. If they can't get their hands on guns, they'll get their hands on another weapon. As evidence of this, all we have to do is take a look at a recent atrocity in China. Guns are illegal there. So what did a perpetrator do? He grabbed a knife and went after a bunch of kindergarten kids, killing 25 of them.

At the other end of the spectrum is the other question: *Should we leave the laws as they are and pray that another mass shooting won't occur?*

The answer to that is also No. Common sense tells us that if we don't fix what's wrong, the matter that's wrong will stay wrong. As a natural consequence, it'll only be a short while before we see another news headline about another senseless slaying.

So what's a society to do?

Instead of entrenching ourselves in one extreme or the other, how about if we explore an area that's somewhere in between? How about if we look towards a neutral setting for the answer?

Currently, the waiting period for a gun purchase according to different state laws is generally 10 days. That means if someone wants to buy a gun so he can walk into a grocery store and shoot everyone in sight, all he has to do is wait 10 days. That means if someone is severely depressed or otherwise psychotic enough to want to commit deadly harm to a bunch of people going about their daily lives, he only has a period of 10 days to overcome his mental vulnerability.

Time heals all wounds. Time can also prevent some fatal wounds. The person wanting to commit a senseless shooting is suffering from a severe mental wound. Why not give him more time to heal from his wound so he won't inflict the pain of his wound upon others?

Why not increase the waiting period for a gun purchase to 1year?

The idea is worth exploring because a lot of good can come out of instituting a 1 year federal mandate.

If someone has lethal intent with his new gun, keeping the gun out of his hands for 365 days can be a life-saver, literally.

A lot of things can happen within that time. The potential perpetrator might accidentally reveal his plans to the people around him, providing them with an opportunity to alert the authorities. The added time frame could give an overworked police department ample opportunity to scrutinize the background of the wannabe gun-owner. Best of all, the calendar year could allow the psychologically damaged person to come to his senses and change his mind. Who knows? He might actually reveal his intent voluntarily to those around him and ask for the help that he needs.

Delaying a gun purchase may not eradicate the sickening trend of violence altogether, but it may slow it down, and from there, we can build on its momentum and improve the well-being of society. In recent memory, these incidents have been happening about once per year. Delaying a perpetrator's gun purchase may reduce that frequency to once every two years. From there, we can start to reverse the trend of senseless violence and make it once every three years, lessening the occurrences that so many copycats need in order to commit their crime. And the lesser these shootings happen, the more we can build a favorable momentum. Perhaps we can all but exterminate the trend, reducing these violent acts down to once every ten years. Think of all the lives we can save and the grief we can prevent by dealing with a random shooting once every ten years instead of once per year.

I can already see some people balking at the idea of having to wait for a full year to buy a gun. I can already see someone who wants to buy a gun for a legitimate reason like deer hunting and not wanting to wait a year before he can go out and shoot some game. For people like that, I can't say I blame them for getting irritated over such a lengthy waiting period. At the same time though, I would have to point out to them that the upside of waiting 365 days clearly outweighs the downside. To this cantankerous bunch, I would say, "If you want to buy a rifle to go deer hunting, won't the deer still be around a year from now?" If they still hemmed and hawed, I would get more candid with my rationale and tell them, "We're all living on borrowed time. Delaying a crazed gunman's purchase of a gun will give some potential victims the chance to borrow another year of life. Is that so outlandish?" Hopefully, that would give them reason to relent. If it didn't, I would proceed to the more-than-candid clincher: "Wouldn't waiting for 365 days be worth **not** coming home one day and finding out that your wife was killed by a crazy gunman while she was shopping for your family's groceries?"

~

Forgive and forget. That can be hard to do. In some instances, it can be impossible. Where it's humanly unattainable, then perhaps the next best thing is to acknowledge and accept. To accomplish that act of reality, it helps to be objective. To be objective, it helps to be neutral.

My personal background is immersed in war. I left Saigon, the former capital of South Vietnam, as a kid without any hatred for the people of North Vietnam etched into my heart. The same cannot be said for many of the adults who fled South Vietnam at the end of the war – like my late father who lost everything he labored so hard to build – twice.

My father was actually born in the northern part of Vietnam and grew up there while the country was still a colony of France. In 1954, when Vietnam won its independence from France after years of fighting, the country was split in two – Communist North Vietnam and Democratic South Vietnam. In the subsequent months, those in the north were given an opportunity to flee to the south if they did not wish to live under a Communist regime. Many seized the opportunity and fled south, abandoning the home and hearth they had built for generations. My father's family was one of those who chose to abandon the land, house, and life they'd built rather than remain under Communist rule.

A civil war ensued.

In 1975, Communist North Vietnam defeated Democratic South Vietnam to lay claim to all of Vietnam. Again, my father couldn't bear to live under a Communist regime, so he abandoned everything he had in South Vietnam and fled with his family to America where he started over from scratch, again.

My late father and many of his generation make up the refugees who have seen and will always see the Communists as a leprous enemy to be despised. Many of them go so far as to lump the children of their former enemy into their heap of hate. They abhor the thought of interacting with today's Vietnam in any way. They are the vanquished who see all of present Vietnam as a nation devoid of any attributes.

I was too busy learning my ABC's while the war was raging. I have never known and will never know the pain my father and his compatriots suffered at the hands of their former enemy. As the saying goes, you have to walk a mile in another person's moccasins to know how they feel. Since that is an impossibility for me, I won't try to ask the generation before me to forgive and forget. I will, however, hold out hope that they will be objective in their views so that they can acknowledge and adjust.

Imagine where society would be today with all of us refused to acknowledge and adjust.

War has been and always will be a part of humankind. War is a deadly contest in which there will be a winner and a loser. War is a vicious fight in which we kill. Some kill to gain. Some kill to keep others from gaining. The land on which all of us live today belongs to either the victor or the vanquished. War, like everything else manmade, has a beginning and an end. If we don't acknowledge that a certain war has come to an end and adjust to that truth, we will at the very least, wallow in an unrelenting rancor.

America is a nation of immigrants. Every immigrant currently inhabiting the contiguous USA is living on land forcibly taken from the American Indians. Every immigrant – including myself – is guilty of living on a land that wasn't originally theirs. It's a fact I can't change and, thankfully, I won't have to change. As tragic as it is, the war between the early settlers and the Indians is over. I don't foresee the Navajos or Cherokees or Iroquois rising up to wage war against all the people living in America to get their land back. There are over 300,000,000 of us living in the United States Of America today, and we don't have any plans on going anywhere else. The Indians have long ago accepted that their land is gone, and that what was once theirs is now ours. While I empathize with them for their loss, I'm also glad they won't take up arms and force me to go live some place else.

Before The United States Of America could become The United States Of America, it had to gain its independence, and that didn't happen without a lot of bloodshed. During the war for independence, George Washington and his armies fought the British. A warning cry that alerted the colonialists to the impending arrival of the enemy was: "The British are coming!

The British are coming!" Think what it would be like if the British refused to accept that they lost the Revolutionary War to the Americans. Imagine what would happen if the Parliament in London today decided to attack America to get their thirteen colonies back. Suddenly, America would be at war with England again, and we would be prone to hearing the warning cry of: "The British are coming – part 2!"

And then there is the Civil War. After five years of bloodletting, the South accepted that the North won and adjusted to that fact. Think of the carnage that the South would create today if it suddenly decided to void the terms of surrender it tendered in 1865 and attacked the North to renew the war.

Today, the majority Vietnam's population was born after the war. They know all too well that the war is in the past and that the Past is but one pillar of the tripod of eternity. They also know that the Past is set in the sedentary stone of time and that it would be an impossible task to try and extract the Past from that unforgiving stone. They're keenly aware that the Present and the Future are the other two pillars they can shapen with much effort. Hopefully, the refugees from yesteryear will adopt a neutral mindset and not obstruct the youth of the Present as they try to construct the pillar of their Future.

Don't Get In The Car With Him

There's a guy I know. His name is "Casey." He has an older brother named "Joe" who's married to "Jennifer," and the couple has a five-year-old son, "Timmy." When Casey graduated from college, he decided to follow the adage advising, "Go west, young man." With high hopes, he packed his bags and prepared to move out to a certain city on the West Coast. As it was, Joe also lived out that way, and Casey's parents recommended that Casey move in with Joe until he got better acclimated to the area. Casey wasn't too enthusiastic about the idea because he and Joe were never two birds of a feather. Whereas Casey was the easy-going type, Joe was hard-headed type, ever ready to declare: "It's My Way Or The Highway!" Despite Casey's reticence, his parents insisted he move in with Joe. Not wanting to rock the boat, Casey moved in with Joe.

In hindsight, Casey made a mistake. That was the bad news. The good news was that Casey's mistake may have been a life saver for Jennifer and little Timmy.

Casey graduated college with a liberal arts degree. Joe was a math and sciences kind of guy. He graduated from college with a solid engineering degree. In Joe's eyes, Casey wasted his money on a wishy-washy degree, and he let Casey know it every time he could, constantly lecturing his younger brother that he squandered his time and money on a useless degree. Casey tried to minimize these arguments, telling Joe that he didn't rely on him in any way and, therefore, didn't want or need any of his lectures. After a month of living under his older brother's thumb, Casey was more than ready to move out. As he later learned, he wasn't the only one wanting to escape from Joe's oppressive domain.

Ever since Casey started living under Joe's roof, he noticed something peculiar. Sometimes, he would see a knife outside Joe and Jennifer's bedroom door. The house was newly built, so Casey just assumed the knife was there for an innocuous reason. Maybe there were bits and pieces of carpeting that needed to be trimmed, Casey thought. Or maybe there was excessive dry paint that needed to be scraped off the walls, he conjectured. Whatever the reason, Casey didn't have any cause to suspect that the knife was there for a malevolent motive.

The young man who never wanted to establish residence with his older brother in the first place also noticed something else. When he sat in the living room and browsed through the newspaper, there were often newspaper cut-outs of handguns for sale on the coffee table. The sight struck him as unusual. Was his brother and sister-in-law planning to buy a gun? Neither of them were gun aficionados, he knew. He couldn't think of why they would want to buy a gun other than a need for home protection.   Was there a rash of break-ins in the neighborhood, he wondered? He didn't think so. The area was nice enough. He was, however, new to the neighborhood, so what did he know? It crossed his mind to ask his brother about the gun ads, and maybe even inquire about the knife outside the bedroom door, but that would involve talking to his older sibling, and doing that would have allowed Joe to launch into yet another corrosive lecture.

Casey considered quenching his curiosity by asking his sister-in-law. That avenue had its own pitfalls though. He and Jennifer got along okay. They were pleasant and cordial enough to one another. Yet, there was an air of unmistakable tension lurking about in the house, like a small, dark animal scurrying from one corner to another. It crossed his mind that the tension may have been the result of his presence in the house. Maybe his sister-in-law never approved of him moving in.   Maybe something was brewing in her mind, and she hadn't voiced it yet. Casey was concerned if he started talking about stuff that was none of his business, his questions might catapult the tension into an unknown territory. He might rock the boat even more, and Casey didn't want to rock the boat any more than he had to. He just wanted to stay under the radar and move out as soon as possible.

That all changed when Jennifer took little Timmy and fled from the house.

Casey had gone to work one Saturday morning to put in some overtime. He came home that afternoon expecting to find the house in its typical atmosphere – uneasy but acceptable. Instead, he discovered that his sister-in-law had packed a bag and taken her son to her parents' house about twenty miles away. He asked his brother what happened. Joe's terse reply was that Jennifer had moved out and taken Timmy with her. When Casey saw that no additional explanation was forthcoming, he gave the matter a very wide berth. Despite his intention to stay clear of the fray, however, Casey couldn't help but learn over the next few weeks that there was much more to the matter than met the eye.

By that point, Joe and Jennifer had been married for about eight years. Sadly, Joe spent much of that time beating his wife. Whenever they had a disagreement – many of which revolved around money and expenses – Joe's method of settling the matter was to hit his wife. Apparently, Jennifer had told her parents and siblings to make them aware of the situation. Unfortunately, she didn't speak a word of it to any of her in-laws. Consequently, no one on Joe's side of the family knew anything about the terrible ordeal. Since they didn't know anything about it, they couldn't do anything about it.

That all changed right after Jennifer ran off to her parents' house.

For whatever reason, Jennifer decided to inform everyone – Joe's side of the family as well as hers – that her husband was beating her and that the assaults had become intolerable. Once the secret was out, Joe's side of the family swung into action and tried to do whatever they could to stop the abuse, especially Joe's mother who made numerous phones calls to her son, crying while imploring him to change his ways. Their effort was valiant. It was also futile.

Joe commanded his wife to come home. She adamantly refused. He went to her parents' house, wielding a knife. He threatened to attack Jennifer and her parents if she didn't return to his house. Jennifer called the police. The officers arrived. They told Joe to go away and stay away. Joe did as they demanded.

Jennifer got a restraining order against Joe. For a while, that did the job, and the chaotic climate calmed down. It was during this time that Casey learned the truth behind the knife outside this brother's bedroom and the newspaper cut-outs of the handguns. To his shock and disbelief, Joe had placed the knife outside the bedroom door and told Jennifer that if she didn't obey his every word, he would stab her and their son to death. To reinforce his threat, he also cut out newspaper ads for handguns and put them on the coffee table, telling Jennifer that he would also buy a handgun and use it to kill Jennifer, Timmy, then himself.

After staying away from her violent husband for about a month, Jennifer thought that it was probably right that her son should see his father, if only for a short period of time. Every Sunday for a few weeks in a row, she drove Timmy back to her house and allowed him to spend a few hours with Joe. That went fine – until Joe decided to change the terms of the visit.

Towards the end of one of Jennifer's weekly visits, Casey was watching TV when Jennifer came into the living room and asked him if he'd seen her car keys. He said he hadn't. She said she could have sworn she left them by the front door, but now she couldn't find them anywhere. She added she was in a hurry to take Timmy back to her parent's house for their Sunday dinner. Casey got up and helped her look for her keys. While searching, he noticed that his brother wasn't participating in the search. Moreover, Joe appeared to be overly nonchalant, standing around in the driveway, contentedly smoking a cigarette.

After an exhaustive search in which Casey and Jennifer looked in the unobvious places as well as the obvious ones, Jennifer became suspicious. She went up to Joe and pointedly asked him if he had taken her keys. He casually replied that he had. Disappointed and irritated yet not terribly surprised, she demanded her keys back. He refused to return her keys and told her she had to stay where she belonged – in his house.

Jennifer said no way. She added that if he wasn't going to return her keys, she would keep looking until she found them. Joe told her not to bother because he flushed them down the toilet.

Jennifer got mad.

Joe got angry.

The two of them got into a heated argument.

Casey looked on with much concern. He recalled the recent revelation that Joe had been beating Jennifer for years. He remembered the knife outside Joe's bedroom door. He remembered the gun ads on the coffee table. He remembered Joe going to his in-laws' house and threatening them. He feared the worst.

Out of nowhere, Joe made Jennifer an offer: "I'll drive you and Timmy to your parents' house."

The offer set off all sorts of alarms in Casey. A second ago, as he was recalling the abuse that Joe had committed, he realized that when Joe was doling out that abuse, he did when no one else was around. As he watched his older brother and wife escalating their argument, he wondered if Joe hadn't laid a hand on Jennifer yet because he was present. That was likely the case, he surmised. His presence was deterring his brother from hitting his sister-in-law.

And now that Joe suddenly offered to drive Jennifer somewhere else could only mean one thing – that he wanted to get Jennifer in a place where he could do as he pleased without any potential interference.

More and more, Casey got the sinking feeling that if Jennifer and her son were to get in the car with Joe, his brother would drive them off to some forsaken place and commit a forsaken act upon them.

While planning for his life after college, Casey often heard people telling him to think of the future. He went ahead and employed that projection now. He looked into his future and saw himself looking back at his past. He saw his future self asking why his past self didn't do what was right. He saw his future self asking why his past self didn't take the necessary actions to get Jennifer and Timmy out of harm's way. Casey didn't want his future to be filled with any regrets. He didn't want to **not** do what was right when he should have. He didn't want to read about a murder-suicide in the next day's newspaper and know it was a tragedy he could have prevented.

"Don't get in the car with him," Casey told Jennifer.

Joe spun around and glared at his younger brother. "Stay out of it!" he demanded.

Casey ignored the warning and repeated to Jennifer, "Don't get in the car with him."

"Huh? What?" Jennifer uttered.

Seeing her confusion, Casey clarified his plan to get her and Timmy out of harm's way. "I'll drive you to your parents' house."

Joe's second warning to his younger brother was as severe as it was succinct: "I said, stay out of it!"

Casey didn't answer. He knew Joe well enough to know that any kind of reply would only spur him on.

By this point, all of them were standing outside in the middle of the driveway. As Casey considered his next step, he wondered if he should go inside and call the cops. He decided against it. Two possibilities could have occurred if he did that. Neither was good.

Now that Joe's anger had gotten the better of him, he might do something to Jennifer the moment Casey stepped away. That was one possibility. The other possibility was an even worse scenario. What if Joe followed Casey into the house to prohibit him from calling the cops? What would happen then?

Would a brawl break out? The phone was only a few steps away from the kitchen where all the knives were. Would the scuffle take an unthinkable, disastrous turn? Casey didn't want to take that chance. He ruled out going inside to call the cops.

Plus, there was another fortuitous factor to consider. As it so happened, Casey already had his car keys in his pocket. Better yet, his car was parked in the street right in front of the house. Casey was literally a few feet from shepherding Jennifer and Timmy into his car and whisking them away. The best course of action was obvious. Casey promptly told Jennifer, "You and Timmy get in my car."

Jennifer was completely onboard with the plan. Without any hesitation, she took her son by the hand, got him and herself into the car, and locked the door. Casey quickly followed suit. He jumped in and started the car.

Raging, Joe started cursing at Casey. "Fuck you!" he yelled. "Fuck you!"

Then, as Casey feared, Joe tried to stop him from leaving with Jennifer and Timmy.

Joe pounded his way into the pavement. He stood in the street, put himself directly in front of Casey's car, and shouted, "You want to take them away? You'll have to run me over! Run me over! I dare you! Run me over!"

Casey looked through the windshield and couldn't believe the spectacle he was seeing. He couldn't believe that his brother was standing in front of his car, blocking his path, daring him to run him over.   The scene was too catastrophic to conceive, yet it was actually happening right before his eyes. Bewildered as he was, Casey recognized the moment called for evasive action, not rueful reflection. He put the car in gear, stepped on the gas – and went in reverse.

He backed up, performing an awkward, reversing sort of U-turn that he barely recalled later when he looked back on the incident with delayed trepidation. Despite the poor aesthetics of his vehicular reversal, Casey managed to get the car pointed away from his furious brother. As soon as he saw a clear path in front of him, he put the car in drive and hurriedly sped away.

Half an hour later, after he had delivered his sister-in-law and her son to safety, Casey questioned what he should do next.

Without a doubt, he knew he couldn't return to Joe's house. He knew that if he was foolish enough to do that, he would assuredly get into a fistfight with his angry brother – if not worse. It was best to steer clear of that foregone conclusion altogether, Casey thought. He mulled over where he should go for the night, and the night after that, and the night after that . . . for he knew he had to stay away from Joe's house permanently – not just for the night. Of all his options, the best one was the home of another relative only a few miles away from the house of Jennifer's parents'. He went over there, told that relative what happened, and asked if he could stay the night. He received the reply he had hoped for, not only for the night, but also for the night after that, and the many, many nights after that.

The following day, while Joe was at work, Casey returned to his brother's house. He went to his small room, quickly threw his few belongings into a box, and unceremoniously exited the house.

When Casey thinks back to this tumultuous event, he's not quite sure himself how he was able to think clearly enough to get his sister-in-law and nephew away from his brother. He's only glad that he was able to maintain a neutral mindset that allowed him to think calmly, clearly, efficiently.

And as result, no harm came to Jennifer and Timmy.

Thanks For Being Late!

Before I continue, I have to pass on another example of how allowing ourselves the benefit of neutral thinking can prevent us from jumping to conclusions.

The airline I work for, like the other prominent airlines in the USA, operates on a hub-and-spoke system. The hubs are major cities like Chicago, Houston, and San Francisco. The spokes are the smaller cities like Albuquerque, Wichita, and Rochester. When passengers wanting to go from a spoke city to a spoke city, such as from Wichita to Rochester, they can't fly nonstop from Wichita to Rochester. They have to connect through a hub like Chicago.

This past winter, I was working a flight from Chicago to Rochester. Once we had boarded the passengers, we were all ready to go, except for the lack of one essential ingredient – the pilots.

Chicago was having one of those bad winter days where the weather was causing lengthy delays. The captain and the co-pilot who were working a flight into Chicago hadn't arrived yet. After half an hour past the scheduled departure time, they still hadn't arrived. After another half an hour, they were still nowhere to be seen. After another half an hour, they finally arrived, and promptly made preparations to take us to Rochester.

The bad part of this delay was that it was a lengthy delay.

The good part of this delay was that many of the passengers flying into Chicago from various spoke cities also arrived late, but since our flight was still there when they arrived, they were able to get onboard our plane and continue to Rochester.

Once the captain gave the signal to close the door, I did as he asked, and we took off for Rochester, arriving there almost 2 hours late.

When the passengers were getting off the plane, the captain and co-pilot joined me at the front door to say good-bye to everyone and thank them for their patronage. Around the middle of the disembarking process, a man approaching the front door said loudly to the captain, "Thanks for being late!"

The captain and co-pilot and I exchanged glances. Based on the face value of the passenger's tone and words, we had to ask ourselves the obvious question: *Was this guy being sarcastic?*

Yet despite that inclination towards a negative interpretation, none of us spouted out a corrosive comeback. This was fortunate because a second later, we learned that the man hadn't intended to be sarcastic at all.

Smiling gratefully, the passenger illuminated the exchange by saying, "I flew from Wichita to Chicago and got in late. If you guys had been on time, I would have missed my connecting flight to Rochester!"

It was then that we fully understood what he meant. The captain gave the man a hearty laugh and told him, "You're welcome!"

I smiled, thankful that the three of us had allowed ourselves a moment of neutral pondering before jumping to the wrong conclusion.

Jumping To Conclusions

While I advocate being neutral since it can help us avoid jumping to conclusions, I have to admit that not being neutral can sometimes have its upside too. Take racial preconceptions, for example.

Our family had a Chinese food restaurant in Winfield, Kansas. (Don't ask why we, a Vietnamese family, opened a Chinese restaurant. That's a whole other story altogether.) Anyway, one sunny afternoon, I was walking from our house to the restaurant that was about a mile away when I heard someone call out, "Excuse me, excuse me!"

I stopped, turned around, and saw a woman waving to me from her front porch. "Yes?" I answered, wondering why this person whom I'd never seen before was calling out to me.

"You want to babysit my kids for me?" she said without any sort of introduction.

I furrowed my brow, unsure if I had heard her right. "Did you say . . . babysit your kids?"

"Yeah," she replied casually. "I got two kids. You want to babysit them for me?"

Since she was to my left and since there was a lawn full of green grass between us, it could be said that her question was coming at me from out in left field. "Um, no thanks," I answered, still digesting the oddity of the request. "I'm not interested in any babysitting."

Disappointment made her voice despondent. "Okay, never mind then."

I started to walk away when the question gnawing on my mind wouldn't let me go: *Why did this woman, a total stranger, ask me to come into her house and babysit her kids for her?*

I had to find out, so I came to a halt and called out to her, "Excuse me."

She had started to go inside but quickly turned around at the sound of my voice. "Yes?" she replied, perking up a little, perhaps thinking I'd changed my mind.

"I'm curious about something . . . we don't know each other . . . why did you ask me to babysit your kids for you?"

"Oh," she answered matter-of-factly, "I heard that you Chinese people make good babysitters!"

Of all the replies she could have given me, that was definitely one I didn't see coming. Struggling to contain my laughter, I said, "Okay. Just curious. Bye."

"Bye," I heard her say as I hurried down the street, turned the corner, and let loose a laugh of enormous proportions.

How the heck did this woman get such a wacky impression, I wondered? I can understand how people might see us "Chinese people" as being good at Kung Fu due to all those Kung Fu movies, but . . . babysitting? How did that happen? I can only guess that I somehow missed a trend. I can only conclude that I must have been comatose during the decade of Chinese babysitting movies. That's how I missed out on the stereotype, and that's how I was caught so off-guard by her reply.

Whatever the reason, this was one instance in which I was glad someone wasn't neutral and wasn't non-assuming. By jumping to a conclusion, the words of that well-meaning woman still gives me a chuckle today.

What Was That?

Around the time that Barry Sanders was winning the Heisman Trophy at Oklahoma State University, I found myself floundering in an ugly incident, one in which I was glad someone in the melee was able to extricate herself and find the right remedy.

It was late in the fall. I remember that because of the darkening, drying leaves dangling from the tree branches — utterly resisting the ultimate fate that had already befallen their brethren lying scattered on the ground. It was also a Friday night, and the students of OSU were hankering to let loose and enjoy the weekend that was at their doorstep. The crowd that I was with was no exception.

Having graduated from high school in Ponca City, a town about an hour north of Oklahoma State University, I came from a school where there were no other Vietnamese students. It wasn't until I started OSU that I started socializing with other Vietnamese people, most of whom came from the larger cities of Tulsa and Oklahoma City. The more I hung out with them, the more I attended their social gatherings. The little party we were having on this autumn night happened to be at a small house that a few of the guys in our group had rented for the school year. As a further happenstance, the house was down the street from a fraternity house.

There were about twenty of us stuffed into that small, weathered abode. Fortunately, most of us were on the small, skinny side and could easily skirt around one another. We lounged about on the worn furniture in the living room and leaned against the walls with the peeling paint as we filled our conversations with the tidbits of college life. With the aroma of "xa xiu" barbeque pork emanating from the oven, I labored with my rudimentary Vietnamese while chatting with the students who were recent arrivals from Vietnam. Unlike the appetizing aroma wafting about the room, the conversations I was having wasn't so free-flowing because of my elementary Vietnamese skills.

I had come to America as a kid and absorbed English so much, so fast, that it had virtually become my first language. Roughly half of the people at the party, on the other hand, didn't come to America until they were well into their teenage years. As a result, they spoke a form of English that was even more faltering than my bad Vietnamese. Despite the obstacles in our linguistics, I felt at ease since it was good to be socializing with the people where I came from. We were all enjoying the pleasant evening until – suddenly – a noise of "bap, bap, bap" disrupted our peaceful setting.

The noise appeared to come from outside the front door.

"What was that?" someone said out loud.

All of us turned towards the door, wondering if the noise was something coincidental, or if it was something that required our attention. The moment passed and, collectively, we dismissed it as insignificant and prepared to return to our little chats, until –

"Bap, bap, bap!"

The sharp noise sounded again.

Coincidence doesn't return so quickly.

One of the girls said it seemed like something was hitting the door. Chinh, a smallish guy in charge of the barbeque pork, came out of the kitchen and said it sounded like someone was throwing rocks at the door. Loi, a stocky guy who had no trouble muscling me out of the paint during our basketball games, opened the door and saw that Chinh was right. There was somebody throwing rocks at our door.

"What are you doing?" Loi called out in accented Vietnamese.

The rest of us rushed to the door to see who he was talking to. We crowded around him and saw that there were three fraternity guys standing in the front yard laughing derisively at us with rocks in their hands.

Chinh squeezed his way to the front door and stood next to Loi. "Why you throw rocks at my door?" he asked the fraternity brothers.

The frat boys answered by cranking up their loud and derisive laughter.

Perplexed, all of us looked on while wondering why these guys were having such a good time throwing rocks at our door.

One of them brought his hand back as if he was going to throw another rock at us.

Someone in our group (I think it was me) flinched.

The perpetrator saw the flinch and laughed. His brothers joined in, and one of them paused in his laughter long enough to call out a taunt we were familiar with: "Ching, chong, choo, chee, chai!"

Then they left.

All of us looked at each other for a second or two, baffled by not only the incident itself but also by the fact that the three uninvited guests went away as quickly as they came. As far as the ethnically insulting part the episode was concerned, we weren't too surprised to see it. Growing up in an area where we were noticeably different, we'd run into that sort of behavior before. As far as their abrupt departure was concerned, however, we didn't really know what to make of it, but since they were gone . . . they were gone . . . so we brushed off the incident as an oddity that we wouldn't have to contend with anymore.

We closed the door and returned to our party.

Around half an hour later, the barbeque pork was done and we were starting to dig in to it when we heard another rapid report of: "Bap, bap, bap!"

Collectively, we jerked our heads towards the door again. This time, we didn't bother to wonder what was causing the sound. We knew it was some frat boys pelting our front door with rocks. One of the braver guys in our group (that's right, it wasn't me) went and opened the door.

Before Loi reached the door, he was visibly irritated and appeared ready to give those three frat guys a serious rebuke.

As soon as he opened the door though, his expression quickly fell from irritated to flabbergasted. Apparently, something that he saw in the front yard had abruptly altered his demeanor. "Damn," we heard him muttering.

As if performing an encore, the rest of us rushed to the door as we did earlier and crowded around behind our impromptu leader. Immediately, we saw why Loi suddenly looked so overwhelmed.

The three frat boys were back. This time, however, they also brought company – lots of company.

Apparently, the fraternity house down the street was having a party of its own. Of course, a frat mixer wouldn't be proper without members of the opposite sex. That's why this fraternity had invited the girls from a sorority house to liven up their gathering. Moreover, it wasn't enough for the fraternity and sorority to enjoy each other's company. They wanted more in the form of entertainment, and their idea of a good time was to give us a bad time.

Evidently, our three original uninvited guests didn't go away and stay away. They went away to spread the word about the fun they were having at our expense, and they invited many of their friends to join in on the revelry. By the looks of the crowd that was in the front yard, virtually everyone at their party had accepted the invitation, and all of them were ready to raise the roof with some raucous racism.

Unexpectedly, a peculiar thought hit me: *Is this what it was like to be black during the early 1900s?*

Although there was no rhyme or reason for me to notch that notation, I couldn't help it. Seeing the mob in front of me, I wondered if this is what it was like to black in the days of extreme segregation. I wondered how it felt to step outside of your house and see a group of people ready to do you harm just because they deemed your skin to be deserving of degradation.

Before I could fathom an answer, the rocks started flying. As before, the rocks weren't big, and they weren't thrown that hard. Even so, they were rocks, and they were being thrown – at us! Although the antagonism wasn't causing us any grievous harm outright, it was antagonism nonetheless. Just as a long journey can start with a single step, mayhem can start with a single moment of malice.

As expected, our group didn't take kindly to being the target of flying rocks. We got mad and advanced.

The fraternity boys advanced as well.

They shouted at us, calling us some names I'd heard before and a few I hadn't. The girls from the sorority house formed a line at the side of the yard, looking very much like a squad of cheerleaders as they merrily shouted the taunts that the original trio had begun: "Ching, chong, choo, chee, chai!"

As much as I want to say I was brave and proceeded to spearhead a defense of our group, I have to admit I wasn't quite at the forefront of the movement. No, I was somewhere towards the back . . . closer to the butt of the spear . . . looking on . . . simultaneously amazed and aghast, fearful and angry, all at once.

Like I mentioned, I'd heard my share of taunts in the past, but this mob mentality that was combining buffoonery and bigotry was a sordid sight I'd never witnessed before.

The next thing I knew, some of the guys from our party did something I didn't see coming at all. They ran past me towards the kitchen, exclaiming: "Get the knives!"

In retrospect, I shouldn't have been surprised they would resort to this. In this fight against the boys from the fraternity house, we were outsized as well as outnumbered. Many of the guys I was chatting with were recent arrivals from Vietnam – a country well versed in the ways of war. To them, a fight was essentially a personal war – and in a war, large or small, personal or otherwise, anything goes. Since we were outsized and outnumbered, they concluded that we had every right to even up the odds. To them, the best way to do that was to get the kitchen knives and turn the utensils into weapons of war.

The sight of the guys I'd been chatting with minutes earlier suddenly running into the house to arm themselves threw me into a state of further dismay. I wanted to tell them to wait a minute. I wanted to tell them to hold on because this

170

wasn't what I signed up for. I came to the party to have a few laughs, not to take part in a few stabbings. Even when we opened the door to find the fraternity boys and sorority girls giving us the one-two punch of taunts and shouts, I didn't envision it getting this far out of hand. I thought there would be a lot of yelling and name-calling, maybe even some pushing and shoving. But that would be the extent of it. I didn't picture any knife fights that would leave someone on the ground bleeding to death.

In hindsight, I should have expected the worst when the rocks started flying. I could tell that the perpetrators invading our front yard were the same ones I walked past everyday on campus. (I think I even recognized one of the guys from one of my classes.) They wouldn't say or do anything to me under normal, everyday circumstances – partly, because they knew to observe the norms of societal constraint and to keep their prejudices to themselves – partly, because they weren't drunk like they are now. Fraternity parties are notorious for their alcohol consumption, and the beer cans some of the guys were waving about readily reinforced that notoriety.

Weighed down by anxiety and alarm, I didn't know what to do – which was why it was good that one of the girls in our group did conjure up the correct course of action. She did what all of us inside the house should have done right away. She saw a disturbance getting out of hand. She heard and saw a lot of shouting along with some pushing and shoving. She saw people running into the kitchen to get the knives. So she kept her wits about her, picked up the phone, and called 9-1-1.

Minutes later (thank goodness it was only mere minutes), sirens sounded the arrival of the policemen. They came to screeching halt in front of the house. The officers got out, sized up the situation, and immediately told everyone to break it up and go back to their respective houses. A few people from each side tried to tell the officers that it wasn't their fault and that it was the other side who started it. The policemen said they didn't care who started it. They said they only cared that all of it came to a stop – immediately!

Everyone saw that the cops meant business. No one wanted to test the officers' demand to disengage and disperse.

Slowly, the sorority girls and fraternity boys trickled back to their mixer, shoveling some sneers at us as they bid a testy retreat.

Seeing that peace had been restored, our group went back inside our house, and the knives were returned to the kitchen drawers.

The rest of the night ended without any fatal fanfare. No more colliding confrontations flared up. No one got stabbed because one of us was, thankfully, neutral-minded enough to call 9-1-1.

Amber Alert

Okay, okay, enough about other people doing things right. Let's get back to me for a second because believe it or not, I'm also capable of keeping calm when the situation calls for it . . . now and then. (Insert some dramatic trumpeting here, pretty please.)

The official job of a flight attendant – contrary to popular belief – isn't to fetch pillows and blankets. It's to provide and maintain safety onboard the plane. Namely, it's to get the passengers out of the airplane in the event of an emergency – ASAP.

Every airline has a system of dealing with an aircraft in crisis at 30,000 feet. Up to a few years ago, my employer used a green light, yellow light, red light system. As the light color indicates, a green light means everything is fine. A yellow light – also known as an "Amber Alert" at my airline – means there's potential trouble ahead. A red light means the trouble has arrived.

On a flight from Los Angeles to Denver, I was the lead attendant – or the flight attendant in charge of the cabin. We took off. I started the service in the First Class cabin. After taking the meal orders and getting an earful from a passenger who didn't get her first choice for her lunch entrée (she got the pasta instead of the chicken), I proceeded to make the drinks.

Unexpectedly, the captain called me on the phone and told me the plane was experiencing a mechanical difficulty. In layman's terms, he said when the airplane takes off, the wing flaps move to a particular position to provide the needed lift. Once the aircraft is airborne and proceeding towards cruising altitude, the wing flaps move to a different position so the airplane can level off and stabilize its altitude. Presently, the flaps on our plane weren't cooperating. They were stuck in their take-off position, causing the plane to keep climbing higher and higher in the sky. Consequently, our malfunctioning flaps were turning our airplane into a rocket.

"Um," I said with growing concern, "is there anything I need to do on my end?"

"Nothing yet," the captain answered. "I'll get back to you in a few minutes."

From my training, I was aware that the captain and co-captain were immediately troubleshooting the issue. They were going through the gamut of dials and gauges in the cockpit to figure out what was wrong. I didn't want to keep the captain on the phone any longer than I had to. "Okay," I replied then promptly hung up.

Obviously, the trouble with the wings had triggered an Amber Alert. I relayed the news to the other flight attendants on my crew. We suspended the beverage service we just started.

Minutes and minutes passed by. Some questions started clamoring in my mind: *Is the captain even coming close to finding a fix? Should I call him and ask him even though my call would interrupt him? Is he in contact with headquarters to find an answer, and if he is, what are they telling him? Should I assume we'll soon be in the red light status at any moment and prepare for a crash landing?*

It was one of those moments where an update from the cockpit – any kind of update – would have been much appreciated. Thankfully, the captain must have heard my silent plea because he called me to apprise me of the situation.

"We're still working on the problem," he said. "We're circling back to Los Angeles as soon as we can. I'll make an announcement to the passengers and let them know what's going on."

As much as I wanted to get more of the details, I didn't want to keep the captain from his urgent duties. Quickly, I said, "Okay," and hung up.

Seconds later, the captain came on the P.A. and informed all the passengers that we were having a mechanical issue with the wings and that he was working on the problem. He added we were returning to LAX and he would keep us updated as much as possible. When he ended his announcement, I expected a rush of questions and comments from the passengers, something like a barrage of: *Did we really hear that right? There's trouble with the wings? Why don't you guys keep better care of your wings? I'm scared as hell! How soon can we get back to L.A.? What's your back-up plan? I want to land now! Is there a back-up plan?*

Surprisingly, I didn't get any of that. On the contrary, I encountered exactly the opposite. No one panicked. No one got bent out of shape. Actually, the whole airplane became extremely quiet. (Even the woman in First Class who was upset that she didn't get her chicken entrée didn't have anything to say, probably because she realized that not getting the chicken wasn't such a big deal after all.)

Years earlier in my flying career – at some junction between having an overly obese woman ask me why her tray table won't come down and hearing a guy tell me he's ready to get off the plane even though we were still taxiing to the gate – I had another mechanical incident on a Boeing 727 that turned out to be a false alarm. Before we learned it was a false alarm, however, the other flight attendants and myself thought it would be best to assume the worst and prepare for the worst. We got out our flight manuals and turned to the section that delineated the steps on how to prepare for a crash landing. Now, with the uncooperative wing flaps threatening to produce a frightful impact, I thought that taking the same precaution would be of help.

The aircraft we were on was a Boeing 757. The other flight attendants and I got out our flight manuals and began reviewing what we needed to do in case the captain called and said the problem was beyond repair and we needed to prepare for a crash landing. Since we train annually for these kinds of predicaments, it didn't take long for us to finalize the actions we needed to take. That was the good part. The uncomfortable part was that we finished so quickly that we had ample time to spare on our hands. With nothing to do but wait for an update from the captain, we stood around and waited.

I'll be the first to admit I was becoming more anxious by the minute. I'll also be the first to acknowledge I had to remain calm – partly because I knew the passengers were looking to me for guidance, partly because I knew the best way to deal with this Amber Alert was to stay calm.

And that acknowledgment proved to be fruitful.

The crew jumpseats are the retractable seats that we flight attendants sit in for take-off and landing. They are, as expected, right by the door to provide for the best facilitation of an evacuation. There were 4 flight attendants working the flight that day. As it so happened, there were also 3 off-duty flight attendants onboard. They were deadheading crewmembers (staff who are traveling as passengers for company purposes) and sitting towards the back of the coach section. I thought ahead and decided that if the plane was going to crash, I wanted to have the best possible odds for survival. The best way to do that, I surmised, was to place the trained professionals at all possible exits in order to get the passengers out as quickly as possible.

The aircraft has 6 doors and 4 windows. Since we had 4 on-duty flight attendants, that meant we could give immediate coverage to 4 of the doors. That left 2 doors and 4 windows without immediate coverage. I had 6 spots to fill, and the 3 additional flight attendants came in very handy.

I called my 3 off-duty colleagues to the front of the plane and told them they were now on-duty. I gave them the details of our staffing and said I needed two of them to cover two of the doors and one of them to cover one of the windows. (In case you're wondering why I gave more importance to the doors, it's because we can evacuate people out of the doors faster than we can out of the windows.) The 3 new additions to the crew gladly pitched in. Two of them filled the two empty jumpseats by the doors, and the third went with me to the window at the overwing exits. (I wished I had three more off-duty flight attendants to fill the other three windows exits, but hey, you work with what you got, right?)

I picked one of the window exits at random and asked the gentleman there to switch seats so that the new on-duty flight attendant could take control of that window. The man's appearance told me he was still shy of his 30th birthday. Politely, he declined my offer and said, "You mind if I stayed here?" He then pointed to the young lady next to him and added, "I'd like my girlfriend and me to be the first ones out."

After mulling over his request, I considered pressing the issue and insisting that he exchange his seat for a trained professional at my side, but I decided against it.

One reason was the factor of time. The captain could call me any minute and tell me the worst case scenario had come to fruition and that I needed to prepare the cabin for a crash landing immediately. If that happened, I didn't have time to argue with a passenger over his seat.

Another reason concerned the mood of the passengers on the plane. The cabin was uncomfortably quiet. The tension was undeniably palpable. I didn't want to make the mood any worse by arguing with a passenger in front of nearly two hundred people.

Yet another reason – and perhaps the most important of them all – was the question of moral rights and the limits of my demand. All of us place a premium on the preservation of life, especially our own lives. If the plane did crash, we would be inside the equivalent of a burning building. Who was I to deny this guy's request to be the first one out of a burning building? He had many decades of life ahead of him. Who was I do deny him his rightful decades?

I acquiesced to his request and turned to the window exit on the other side of the aisle. Before I could finish even posing my question to the woman sitting there, she gladly got out of the seat and gave it to the flight attendant standing next to me. Apparently, she didn't mind giving up the task of evacuating an airplane to a trained professional.

Having installed the last of my helper flight attendants, I went to the back and reviewed the situation with my two of my crewmembers back there. They were more experienced than I was. I wanted to get their input and see if I had missed anything. When they said they couldn't think of anything else, I returned to the front and waited for a call from the captain.

While waiting, I made myself a cup of coffee. Hoping to portray a picture of composure to help calm the anxiety I knew was building up in the passengers, I made it a point to stand at the front of the plane, in the middle of the aisle, while leisurely sipping my coffee. Did my portrayal of composure have any effect on the passengers? I have no idea. I only knew at the time that it couldn't hurt, and anything that couldn't hurt could have been of help.

So while the entire airplane simmered in a discomforting silence, I sipped my coffee and waited for an update from the captain.

And I waited . . .

. . . and waited . . .

. . . and waited . . .

. . . and waited . . .

. . . until . . . the captain called!

"We fixed the wings," he said to the delight of my ears. "We'll be landing at LAX soon. Go ahead and prepare the cabin for landing."

"Will do," I quickly assented.

"Oh, one more thing," he hastily added. "After we land, we won't be able to turn off the runway. It's an issue with steering. Long story. We'll go to the very end of the runway and get hooked up to one of those tug vehicles, and they'll pull us in to the gate."

An issue with the steering? That didn't sound good. And we would need to get tugged in to the gate? That was strange. Was there more that I should know about? Again, I didn't want to keep the captain from his duties, so I didn't ask. If he said we would be safely landing soon, then I'm happy to go along with that prospect. If there was a steering problem, I wouldn't mind at all dealing with that after we're on the ground.

I relayed the captain's message to the rest of the crew then announced to the passengers that we would be landing soon at LAX. As we typically do prior to landing, the rest of the staff and I walked through the cabin to make sure the passengers had fastened their seatbelts, stowed their tray tables, and brought their seatbacks upright.

It was around this time that I realized I could have done something additional while waiting for the captain to call with an update. Before every flight, we play a safety video that calls attention to the exits. Since there was a chance that an emergency evacuation would be necessary, I should have played that video again to refresh the passengers' knowledge of the exits. I made a mental note of this for future reference, although to be perfectly honest, I hope my future will never need this kind of reference.

Minutes later, we landed and proceeded to the end of the runway where a tug vehicle hooked us up and pulled us to the gate. Everything went smoothly. For an unplanned event, everything worked out as planned.

When the gate agents opened the door, a team of supervisors came onboard and asked if everyone was okay. The captain also stepped out of the cockpit and asked if everyone was okay. All of us said we were okay.

The passengers stepped off the plane and got their flights rebooked.

We flight attendants kept going with our work schedule.

Later on, a supervisor gave me a written commendation for my actions. (Somehow, it got pasted into this book, at the end of this segment. I have no idea how it got there, huh-uh, not a clue.) I accepted the accolade with gratitude, only too glad I was able to find my neutral zone and come up with a strategy, and only too relieved I didn't have to fully execute that strategy.

```
10-23-11/COMPANY COMMENDATION              /MARIE          /
FT:   558/ID:1046/DY:.../TM:..:../HR:...:../DT:102111
      PER LAXSW BESTY*OUTSTANDING RESPONSE TO AMBER     /
      ALERT                                             /
```

My Foibles

Although I've pointed out some of my foibles thus far, the truth is I've erred more than what I've admitted to. I'd say that for about every one instance in which I succeeded at neutral thinking, I've failed five times more. It's only right that I come clean about all of my debacles. It's only right that I confess to all of my blunders. Before I do that, however, allow me to indulge in a moment of hubris and relay to you how my neutral thinking probably saved our family a bundle of money.

Around 2005 or so, my siblings and I were discussing the prospect of moving our aging parents from Kansas to Southern California so they could be closer to a network of relatives. As you may know, the cost of housing in Southern California isn't cheap. To make matters worse, the housing market was rocketing into the stratosphere, and the run-of-the-mill houses were commanding outrageous prices. In our blue-collar neighborhood, for example, a small house measuring about 1,000 square feet was going for $600,000.

That was an unbelievable increase of 300%!

Anyone applying the basic economic rule of supply and demand could easily see that this enormous price hike didn't make sense. Only two conditions could have warranted the runaway price of this house and thousands of others like it.

From the perspective of supply, the number of houses in the area had to have *decreased* by 300% to justify the exorbitant jump price tag. It hadn't.

From the perspective of demand, the population had to have *increased* by 300% to justify the exorbitant price tag. It hadn't.

So what was causing the outlandish marketplace mark-up?

Simply put: *Greed.*

As all of us now know in retrospect, it was a housing bubble that would eventually trigger the Great Recession.

At the time, I didn't recognize it as a bubble. To say that I did would have been giving myself too much credit for insightful economic knowledge. Despite that prowess, however, I did have the common sense to say to my siblings, "Hold on. Something's not right."

My brothers and sisters and I were going to pool our money together to buy a house for our parents. As the price of the houses in Southern California climbed higher and higher, I became more and more nervous at the financial pitfalls that lay ahead of us. What if, I posed in one of our group emails, we bought a house and the price dropped precipitously a few years later? What if we paid $600,000 for a house only to see its value plummet to $200,000 in five years?

That means we would have lost $400,000!

In my eyes, that was way too big of a risk. Let's wait, I proposed. The housing market was just too crazy, and I didn't want us losing a bundle because we bought at a crazy time.

The reaction I got was mixed. Some of my siblings were as reticent as I was. Some were bullish and wanted to march forward undeterred. The latter group contended that housing in Southern California would always be high in demand and that we could always sell later at a higher price. This assumption didn't sit well with me. Even if we were able to sell at a higher price at a later date, what if that price was much lower than the price we paid for the house? The net result would be a loss for us. The best course of action, I advocated, was to wait for the frenzied market to settle down. The prudent projection, I maintained, was to stay put and do nothing.

Thankfully, that's what we eventually did. We stepped back. We stayed neutral. We let the fever of the housing market run its course.

When we finally bought a house, we paid hundreds of thousands of dollars less than the price at the height of the bubble. Looking back at it now, I'm happy to say that I was one of the voices that said to let the market neutralize itself before we made a purchase.

Now that I've sufficiently patted myself on the back and gotten that self-accolade out of the way, let me tell you about all the episodes where I failed to be neutral and, consequently, fell flat on my face. First, there was . . . . oh, my goodness . . . would you look at that?

We've run out of paper! There's no more room for me to tell you all the things I did wrong! I'm so sorry!

I'll tell you what. I'll do my utmost to bare my soul in a sequel and divulge every instance where I wasn't neutral and erred exponentially as a result? There will be so many anecdotes in that sequel that it will be a work of encyclopedic proportions.

Until the publication of that tome, please remember this: *If you find yourself in a predicament of any kind, don't dive headlong into the extremes*. Find a calm state. Stay objective. Explore a neutral solution.

Strive for that, and you're bound to discover **The Benefits Of Neutral Thinking**.

Made in the USA
Coppell, TX
20 November 2019

11624434R00105